ADVANCE PRAISE

"The difference between entrepreneurs who make it and those who don't is the ability to execute, adapt, persevere, and surround themselves with talent. This book is the difference-maker, packed with solid strategies and sound advice to help you ride the startup roller coaster. There are plenty of books that talk about starting a new venture. This one is the complete manual and will be a well-worn reference guide to help you along your journey."

—CHRIS SHIPLEY, ENTREPRENEUR, MENTOR, AND AUTHOR OF *THE ADAPTATION ADVANTAGE*

"This book is a must-read for any entrepreneur serious about succeeding. Maria distills her success into methods to help you execute, adapt, persevere, and find the right people to be on your rocket ship."

—LAURA KILCREASE, CEO OF ALBERTA INNOVATES AND MANAGING DIRECTOR AND FOUNDER OF TRITON VENTURES

"I've watched Maria Flynn create opportunities for fifteen years, and now she shares her insights with you. This book is an inspiring, how-to-get-it-done resource for entrepreneurs by an experienced entrepreneur."

—JOE HADZIMA, GLOBAL CHAIRMAN OF MIT ENTERPRISE FORUM AND MANAGING DIRECTOR OF MAIN STREET PARTNERS

"For anyone mentoring founders, Make Opportunity Happen is a resource to pass on to those entrepreneurs looking to move their companies forward."

—RYAN MORLEY, SERIAL CO-FOUNDER, INVESTOR, AND PARTNER AT SPRINGTIDE VENTURES

"If you want to make more progress before you run out of time and money, read Maria Flynn's Make Opportunity Happen. You'll find practical, actionable methods to help you get it done."

—STARR MARCELLO, DEPUTY DEAN FOR MBA PROGRAMS AND ADJUNCT ASSOCIATE PROFESSOR OF ENTREPRENEURSHIP AT THE UNIVERSITY OF CHICAGO BOOTH SCHOOL OF BUSINESS

"Make Opportunity Happen coaches you on how to simplify and get things done. All entrepreneurs need this book by their side."

—DAVYEON ROSS, THREE-TIME FOUNDER AND INVESTOR

MAKE OPPORTUNITY HAPPEN

MAKE
Opportunity
HAPPEN

THE ENTREPRENEUR'S GUIDE
TO ALIGN YOUR OWN STARS

MARIA FLYNN

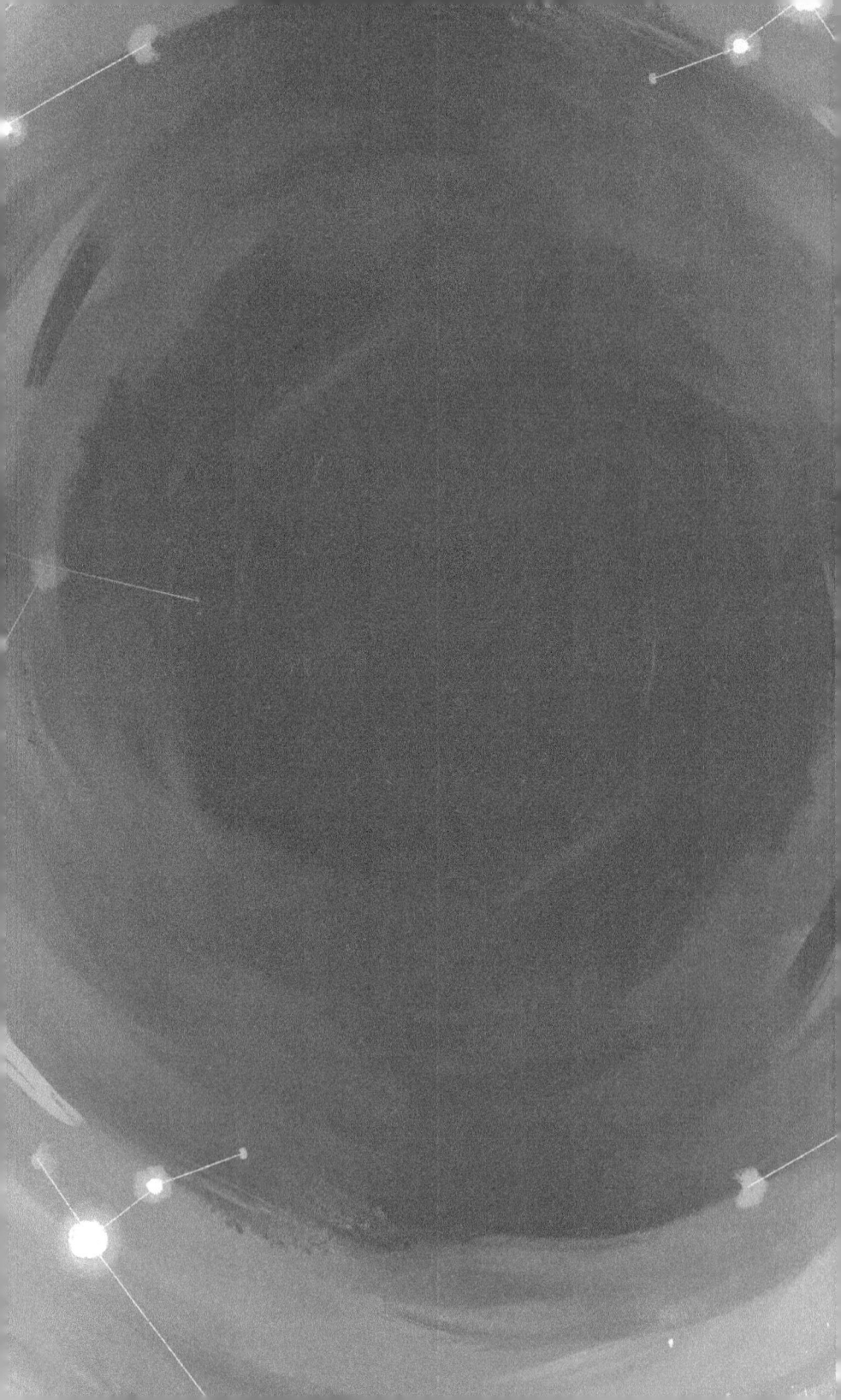

LIONCREST PUBLISHING

COPYRIGHT © 2024 MARIA FLYNN
All rights reserved.

NO AI TRAINING: Without in any way limiting the author's exclusive rights under copyright, any use of this publication to "train" generative artificial intelligence (AI) technologies to generate text is expressly prohibited. The author reserves all rights to license uses of this work for generative AI training and development of machine learning language models.

MAKE OPPORTUNITY HAPPEN
The Entrepreneur's Guide to Align Your Own Stars

FIRST EDITION

ISBN 978-1-5445-4548-6 *Hardcover*
 978-1-5445-4547-9 *Paperback*
 978-1-5445-4546-2 *Ebook*

Contents

MOVING YOUR STARS INTO POSITION..................15

PART 1: EXECUTION CONSTELLATION

1. YOUR MIGHTY MINDSET............................... 27
   Develop a mindset that propels you.

2. VALUABLE VS. VICIOUS VOICES..................... 35
   Identify your voices and put them to work for you.

3. THE MAGIC OF MOMENTUM 43
   Recognize it's all about taking the first step and keeping momentum going.

4. KNOWING WHERE YOU WANT TO GO....................51
   Establish your destination and align every person on your team's goals to the overarching mission.

5. THE RIGHT THINGS RIGHT NOW 59
   Leverage key performance indicators (KPIs) to work on the right things.

6. WHAT TO WORK ON TODAY 67
   Break larger goals into bite-size tasks along multiple paths so you can make the most progress.

7. ACCOUNTABILITY FOR YOU AND YOUR TEAM 73
   Have a system and discipline to get things done to increase your accountability.

8. ACCOUNTABILITY FOR YOUR CLIENTS AND PARTNERS 79
   Bring a set of golden rules to help you increase accountability.

9. URGENCY BUILDERS 87
   Create urgency so you don't have the "in six months" problem.

10. EMPOWERED DECISIONS 95
    Use your framework of what is important to make good, quick decisions.

PART 2: SUPPORT CONSTELLATION

11. MANAGING OVERWHELM 105
    Give yourself a time audit and a three-step plan to manage your overwhelm.

12. ROLLER-COASTER SURVIVAL 115
    Use this checklist to help you put things into perspective.

13. YOUR ROCKET SHIP 121
    Think strategically about your team, common characteristics to share, and diversity of experience and skills.

14. FOUNDER AND CO-FOUNDERS 127
    Decide your leadership structure, align expectations, and have a plan for how to work together.

15. CLARITY OF STRUCTURE 137
    Define who does what to improve accountability and team dynamics.

16. CULTURE CORNERSTONE 143
    Use the golden rule, treating people the way they want to be treated, as a cornerstone of your culture.

17. THE WAY WE WORK 149
    Define how you do things, so everyone is on the same page.

18. HIRING BASICS 155
    Recruit the best people you can.

19. YOUR BOARD 165
    Identify, set up, and run a board that propels your company.

20. FRIENDSHELP 175
    Get by with a little help from your friends.

PART 3: ADAPTABILITY CONSTELLATION

21. MONKEY MIND 187
    Tame your restless mind, reduce anxiety, and capture insights.

22. FREEING YOUR FEELINGS 195
    Let your emotions help you rather than hinder you.

23. CREATIVITY CATCHERS 203
   Get into the creative zone and capture your ideas.

24. LISTENTUITION 211
   *Look for the green lights for encouragement
   and the speed bumps for learning.*

25. RAPID DISCOVERY 219
   Experiment to find answers quickly.

26. YOUR STORY 229
   Tell your best story and adapt it to the right audience.

27. NEGOTIATION STARTER PACK 237
   *Practice negotiation skills so both parties
   feel good about moving forward.*

28. THE RIGHT STRUCTURE AT THE RIGHT TIME 245
   Work on the right things at the right time.

29. LETTING SOMEONE GO 251
   *Be thoughtful in firing as it reflects on the type of
   leader you are and the company you have.*

30. FAILING UP 259
   *Maximize the value of failing by learning
   from and moving on from it.*

PART 4: PERSEVERANCE CONSTELLATION

31. SHIT HAPPENS 269
    Have a plan so you and your team can recover faster.

32. MAKE OPPORTUNITY KNOCK 277
    *Find ways to increase the potential for
    opportunity to come your way.*

33. GETTING INTO DOORS 283
    *Perfect the first step in selling your product,
    service, idea, or company.*

34. FUNDING 291
    *Consider revenue, grants, angel funding, and venture
    capital when finding what funding fits you best.*

35. GET UNSTUCK 301
    *Take action and learn quickly, and the
    market will tell you the way to go.*

36. AVOIDING THE STRESS OF NOT GETTING
    THINGS DONE 309
    *Avoid the dangers of putting too much on your
    list with strategies for preventing overload.*

37. WHAT FILLS YOU UP 317
    Do more of what gives you energy and less of what drains you.

38. THE "LONG IN THE TOOTH" SYNDROME 325
    *Keep your business from getting old where you are
    continually asking yourself, Is this worth it?*

39. YOUR NEXT WIND 333
   Find renewed energy by hitting the reset button; making adjustments to your routines, habits, and environment; or making a change.

40. LEANING ON OTHERS 339
   Embrace your tribe to provide and receive inspiration, support, and ideas.

   CONCLUSION: WELCOME, SHOOTING STAR 345

   ACKNOWLEDGMENTS 349

Moving Your Stars into Position

BEFORE HE CHANGED THE WORLD, NO ONE TOOK HIM SERIOUSLY. Julio Palmaz moved to the United States to pursue medical research. He saw the need for a scaffold to keep the heart vessel open after the balloon angioplasty procedure, used as a heart treatment. Julio envisioned a tube-shaped device that surgeons would insert into the heart's arteries to keep the artery open, so he researched implantable metals and made prototypes in his garage. His eureka moment arrived when Julio found a piece of metal lathe on the floor and thought this was what he was searching for. And that little piece of metal set him on the path to inventing the first balloon-expandable heart stent.

Julio approached several companies with his invention. They all turned him down. He encountered naysayers at his university too. He was even criticized when he disclosed his invention to the patent review committee. They asserted it would never work and that no one was going to put metal in their body. Julio seemed to be at a dead end.

The investors also turned him down. But ironically, a wealthy restaurateur was interested. It turns out that an expert in hamburgers and pasta could see the promise in Julio's vision. Julio to help you make things happen so you can say, "Look how we are lining up our stars!"

This book is about aligning your stars, which means your business is fulfilling your intended vision. It's having an impact, reaching the customers, growing the revenue, and realizing the vision of why you started your business in the first place.

How do you know when your stars align? These are some clues:

- Profitability
- Happy clients, happy employees, and happy you
- Growing excitement to find out what happens next

So, how do you know when stars are "aligning"? When the world gives you feedback that you are going in the right direction, you are *getting* your business to this result. You are metaphorically moving heavenly bodies around—adjusting your mindset, doing these methods, using these templates—so that your business starts taking the shape you want. Aligning your stars is an ACTIVE process, which starts by following the methods and templates in this book.

Make Opportunity Happen: The Entrepreneur's Guide to Align Your Own Stars is an entrepreneur's manual for making things happen from someone who has been through it. This book brings you methods and templates to get things done. Through my own journey, I often "took a page" from my entrepreneurial heroes and friends' playbooks, and in these pages I pass them on to you. You don't want to recreate the wheel. You learn from others any chance you get.

There are key *constellations* you must align to find success with your venture. Beyond the astronomy and astrology definitions of a constellation, you see this definition:

Constellation [kon-stuh-ley-shuhn]
Noun
A group or configuration of ideas, feelings, characteristics, objects, etc., that are related in some way. A constellation of qualities that made her particularly suited to the job.

The thesaurus gives these synonyms:

"as in pattern"—kind, method, sequence, pattern
and
"as in destiny"—future, objective, intention, prospect

Your *constellations* are the *methods* that help create your *future*. These constellations allow you to move your stars in the direction you want. For entrepreneurs, the important constellations are execution, support, adaptability, and perseverance. This book focuses on these four constellations:

1. **Execution.** It's the ability to make things happen to create something beautiful. You need to know how to move your stars into place. Smart, timely action gets you there.
2. **Support.** The people around you form the structure to align your stars. No one does it alone. You need enough internal and external support to get you where you want to be.
3. **Adaptability.** Heavenly bodies move, and so must you. Evolution is vital for entrepreneurs.
4. **Perseverance.** It's the strength to keep going and find ways to move your stars in the direction you need them to go. Entrepreneurship is a long game. Perseverance is required.

This book focuses on these constellations in your journey,

and each part includes the most important stars or methods for each constellation. Mindset permeates your experience and is incorporated into the first two methods of the constellations. Each constellation has ten methods covering important topics for early-stage entrepreneurs, totaling forty methods. In biblical history, "the number forty" is used as a time of testing, difficulty, and wandering in the desert. Appropriately, then, the forty methods in *Make Opportunity Happen* will help you navigate the difficult entrepreneurial experiences, which will test your faith, but which also will strengthen your desire to complete what you've started.

The methods give you a primer on essential topics entrepreneurs need to know, like recruiting, establishing the way you work, and getting unstuck. You'll learn approaches to accountability and building urgency. There will be methods that speak to you now and others that you will refer to later. Everyone is going through things at a different time, and the goal is to have starting points for you with the right information at the right time. It's best to read the book quickly and then refer to the methods as you need them. The "Where to Find What You Are Looking For" guide lets you jump to a particular area you are dealing with.

Each method has a template to put the ideas into practice. Check out the website makeopportunityhappen.com for downloadable, editable templates. Use the forms as a way to fast-track your thinking on these topics.

There are entire books that cover many of these topics, especially funding, selling, and mindset. My goal is to provide you with primers based on a few decades of the things I wish I'd known when I started my entrepreneurial journey. These methods get you started, and when you're ready for a deeper dive, you have a curated selection of resources for more information when needed.

These resources, and the way they're structured, is the product of much thought and reflection. This is a book for busy entrepreneurs, and the book I desperately needed on my own entrepreneurial journey.

There are no magical answers here. This is a set of methods and templates to help guide you to your own solutions. Many books have wonderful ideas that sound great but don't give you guidelines for putting the ideas into practice. In this book, each method provides templates to answer your *Now what?* question and additional resources if you have time to dive deeper.

HOW I GOT TO BE YOUR GUIDE

Growing up on a Kansas wheat farm, you don't run down the street and knock on someone's door to see if they can play. My closest friend was 2.1 miles away via highway. You learn to be independent, resourceful, and proactive because you see other people around you who can do practically anything. Oh, that motor doesn't work? Get the parts and fix it. Oh, that fence has a hole in it? Get the tools and repair it. I saw this attitude in my parents, grandparents, and brothers. Luckily, the mindset rubbed off on me, and translated later in my life: Oh, you need to run a biotech? Figure it out and do it. Farm training sets the stage for a great entrepreneur's toolbox.

My parents had farm, real estate, architecture, and interior design businesses, and their kids played a part in them. We talked about business around the dinner table and had jobs in these businesses in the summer and after school. Growing up with entrepreneurial conversations prepares you to become an entrepreneur.

As a kid, I planned to be a ballerina or an interior designer when I grew up. But my "practical" DNA instilled by generations of farmers led me into engineering. I loved the business side of technology, where innovation meets opportunity. I loved the thrill of the hunt, and engineering gave me the foundation to hunt for many possibilities. An engineering mindset trained me to think with both structure and creativity.

From my engineering launchpad, I became an entrepreneur. First, inside a large company, Cerner Corporation, we were developing the next new technology. Later, I was the CEO of Orbis Biosciences, a pharmaceutical manufacturing technology company. Orbis made drugs safer and longer lasting. I journeyed from startup to selling Orbis to a large manufacturer, Adare Pharma, and learned many lessons.

Since Orbis, I have worked with over thirty companies, helping entrepreneurs align their stars. I did this as the Managing Director of Techstars Kansas City and through my consulting company, Ambiologix. In all my work, I seek to help entrepreneurs simplify, focus, and form the right questions. These lessons and methods have proven effective across industries from health tech, biotech, and deep tech into other sectors like marketing, financial services, and consumer products.

Thinking back over my life makes me wonder if I might have taken the same journey if my parents weren't entrepreneurs. What about all the business founders exploring this world for the first time? What if this is your first startup, and you haven't had the opportunity to ride along with thirty other companies? How do you level the playing field?

With the methods and templates in *Make Opportunity Happen*.

You don't need to wait for the stars to align. These strategies can enable you to move your own stars into place. Let's get started!

PART I

Execution Constellation

"It always seems impossible until it is done."
—NELSON MANDELA

YOUR EXECUTION CONSTELLATION IS YOUR ABILITY TO MAKE things happen to create something beautiful. The best ideas without execution keep you grounded without liftoff or spinning your wheels and never getting to your destination. You need to focus on the methods that hone your execution.

The mindset methods establish your Mighty Mindset and use your Valuable Voice while controlling your Vicious Voice. Leverage the magic of momentum at each step of the journey by knowing where you want to go, understanding the right things to do right now, and knowing what to work on today. Accountability and Urgency Builders are key to execution. Knowing what's important to you helps you make empowered decisions.

METHOD 1

Your Mighty Mindset

"Believe you can, and you're halfway there."
—THEODORE ROOSEVELT

ORBIS BIOSCIENCES' OWNERS PLANNED TO BUILD ORBIS AND sell the company to a large manufacturer, and we intended that journey to take three to five years. We made it to exit in twelve years. But we'd actually believed the timing was right a few years prior, when we'd run an exit sales process with an investment banker. We had successfully scaled the technology and were nearing important licensing deals. In our market research, we heard things from potential buyers like, "We will bid and not be outbid." While we did get one letter of intent, it was clear that this was not our time to exit. We needed to keep going. It was a huge bummer because the sales process, with its hundreds of hours diverted from our core business and the emotional investment, had taken so much out of us, and we didn't cross the finish line.

Everyone deals with loss differently. Your mindset is either the single biggest thing moving you forward or the single biggest thing holding you back. Even within the same week, I have days I know that I either win or I learn (and thus, I win), and

clients, but it also seems less important when you take your key learnings and move on to the next, even better client.
- Let it go. You try to control everything. There is freedom in knowing that the outcome is beyond our control. It doesn't mean giving in. It means doing what you can in a world that meets you on its terms. If you are smart and diligent and develop good strategies, the world will inevitably meet you. It just might not meet you in the place you expected.

To move toward a Mighty Mindset:

- Have two to three go-to lines that get your mind where you want it to be. Move your thoughts from negative to positive, doubtful to hopeful, and backward-looking to forward-looking. Two lines I use often are *Spiral Up!* and *What's the worst thing that will happen?*
- Take a page from the athletes who visualize their actions and see themselves performing as they want to perform.
- Listen to music that gets you into the right mindset.
- "Power Pose!" Watch Amy Cuddy's talk on the importance of physical posture to your success.
- Practice, practice, practice. Practice in front of the mirror, recording yourself, and in front of friends and colleagues, usually in that order.
- Have empowering rituals. Practice a morning power hour, exercise routines, bedtime reviews, and self-care sessions.
- Go back to your why. What is your purpose? Why does your company exist?

Using these methods helps you build confidence, conviction, and commitment.

A Mighty Mindset keeps you moving forward.

YOUR *mighty* MINDSET

(1)

PEOPLE
_____
_____
_____

FUEL
_____
_____
_____

EXTERNAL SUPPORT SYSTEM

INTERNAL SUPPORT SYSTEM

MY FAVORITE PHRASES...
_____
_____
_____

TO USE WHEN...
_____
_____
_____

ENVIRONMENT
_____
_____
_____

EXPERIENCES
_____
_____
_____

Template Notes

You can download a printable version of this template at: makeopportunityhappen.com/templates/01

In the center of the circle, map your **internal support system**: your go-to **phrases** and **when** you're going to use them. For example, I remind myself to "Spiral up" when I catch myself complaining.

In the outer ring, map your **external support system**: the **people** you go to for support, the **fuel** that nourishes you (like podcasts, music, and books), the **experiences** that sustain you (like exercise, hobbies, and self-care), and the things in your **environment** that boost you (like images, sounds, smells, and tastes).

RECAP

The top four ways to use a Mighty Mindset to align your stars:

1. Develop, train, and maintain your mindset muscle. You get to choose your mindset, so make it intentional.
2. Use gratitude, take the first step, and let go as methods to adjust your mindset.
3. Find the go-to methods that help you adjust your mindset.
4. Map your external and internal support systems in Template 1, and refer to this when you need support.

RESOURCES

- *Mindset: The New Psychology of Success* by Carol Dweck
- *The Hard Thing About Hard Things: Building a Business When There Are No Easy Answers* by Ben Horowitz, Kevin Kenerly, et al.

- *Start with Why: How Great Leaders Inspire Everyone to Take Action* by Simon Sinek and his TED Talk
- *Presence: Bringing Your Boldest Self to Your Biggest Challenges* by Amy Cuddy and her TED Talk

※ ※ ※

When working in your Execution Constellation, your Mighty Mindset is the first place to start. It's your foundation. Part of developing a mindset that propels you is managing your voices. You should leverage your *Valuable Voice* and control your *Vicious Voice*. Let's dive into that next.

METHOD 2

Valuable vs. Vicious Voices

> "The most important conversation you're ever going to have is the conversation you're having with yourself."
> —SHANNON L. ALDER

IF YOU HAD MET ME IN GRADE SCHOOL, YOU WOULD HAVE thought I wouldn't grow into much. I was quiet, small, and sporting the perpetual 1980s perm. My invisible strengths were a fierce work ethic, the ability to figure things out, and a healthy belief in myself. My parents and brothers would say, "Yeah, go for it!" While they may have harbored questions about how it would turn out, they never let it show.

It wasn't until my early thirties when my mom told me, "There you go again, aiming for something you won't get. Then, somehow, you get it." When I heard my mom say this, I was glad I had never known she felt this way until I was in my thirties. I always worked on self-confidence, but I had this deep faith and belief that I could figure things out.

It doesn't matter how good your methods are if you don't believe you will get there. It's the famous Henry Ford quote: "Whether you think you can, or you think you can't—you're right." Mindset is deep-rooted in your beliefs, values, and actions. Adjust your mindset to make it possible for you and your team to get things done.

Many people don't move forward because of their self-talk. The things you tell yourself are critical to *Make Opportunity Happen* in the Execution Constellation. Acknowledge that what you tell yourself is important. Incorporate what you want to tell yourself as part of your morning routines, evening routines, and everything in between.

Hopefully, you are fortunate to have a list of people cheering on your sideline. But even if you don't, the strong internal voice crushes doubt from within and outside. What is your pep talk? My pep talk is looking in the mirror and telling myself, "You've got this. Go get it done." Master yours.

To manage your voices, you have to be good at giving yourself pep talks. Your pep talk is what you tell yourself to psych yourself up. This is especially important when things aren't going how you want them to, you are tired, and that negative voice starts to pop into your head. Your pep talk refocuses you in the direction you want, gives you a second wind, and quashes those negative voices.

You sometimes don't notice how often your negative voice speaks because it has been with you for so long. This is the bully's voice, the *Vicious Voice*. Your Vicious Voice says things like:

- *Why can't I catch a break?*
- *Should I be doing this?*
- *Is this impossible?*
- *Am I ever going to make it?*
- *I'm not _____ enough.*

Now ask yourself:

- *Who gets to decide the answers?*
- *What is my narrative of myself?*
- *What evidence do I have of this narrative?*

What do you say about yourself to others, particularly your most trusted inner circle? Those are the grooves that you are wearing in your mind. Limiting beliefs are so programmed in us that it's difficult to know they are there. They are sneaky suckers. For a few decades, I told myself I was the slow-starter, strong-finisher type. At least I gave myself the strong-finisher part. Then, recently, I asked myself, *What evidence do I have to back up the slow-starter belief?* Yes, I was a small kid and late to grow, but that is all the data I came up with. I saw this belief manifest in negative ways. When I started writing this book, for example, I told myself, *I'm sure the book won't be that great, but I am a hard worker, so I know I'll improve.* Why didn't I tell myself, *I know the book will be great because it's my favorite topic that I know a lot about?* I was letting myself start from a position of weakness by letting this slow-starter thought linger as a limiting belief.

Look for the positive voice inside you—the one that tells you, *Go for it, you've got this*—and *don't worry about what anyone else thinks*. That voice is your *Valuable Voice*. Become friends with your Valuable Voice. How many friends you have on your sideline matters less than the friend you have within yourself. The problem is that sometimes, you let the Vicious Voice overpower the Valuable Voice.

You have to be your own biggest cheerleader. If you aren't using your Valuable Voice, then your Vicious Voice gets the airtime. You can't expect others to be any more pro-you than you. How's your self-talk? Are you kind to yourself? Awareness of your self-talk and regularly evaluating what it tells you is important. Would you tell your friend the things you say to yourself? If not, why do you tell yourself this? When you realize you talk to yourself much worse than you would talk to your friends, you have an opportunity to fix it. Watch what you say to your friends, and then give your internal friend permission to say those things to yourself.

Often, you let your mind control the narrative rather than directing the narrative. Template 2 helps you distill what you tell yourself. Consider common things you say and put them in the useful or limiting categories. If this is new, you need time to realize what you tell yourself. If you keep the page beside you, you'll see, *Yeah, I tell myself that a lot.* Or *There I go again, telling myself I'm not good enough.* Or *That helped when I told myself, "Screw it. I don't care what he thinks."* Do that more.

Once you determine what is useful, find ways to reinforce it. How can I say these positive things more? Post the phrase on your computer. Attach the phrase to a certain behavior. For example, when you start complaining, think about something you are grateful for.

List specific experiences that serve as tangible evidence of your achievements. This gives substance to the "I've got this!" self-talk. You know you've got this because you have proved it many times. You need to pause to remember that you've done it before.

Once you decide what is not helpful, find ways to counteract it. Whenever I start to doubt if I'll ever finish this project, I'll remind myself how far I have come.

Managing your voices is about identifying your Valuable and Vicious Voices, stopping the Vicious Voice, and putting your Valuable Voice to work for you.

VALUABLE vs. VICIOUS VOICES

MY SELF-EVALUATION: WHAT DO I TELL MYSELF?

USEFUL PHRASES:

LIMITING PHRASES:

MY EXERCISE PLAN: WHAT DO I WANT MY AUTOMATIC NEXT STEPS TO BE?

REINFORCERS:

COUNTERMEASURES:

Template Notes

You can download a printable version of this template at: makeopportunityhappen.com/templates/02

In the top section, write phrases you tell yourself that are **useful** to help you move forward, and phrases that **limit** you from moving forward. Notice patterns or recurring themes.

For the helpful phrases, what **reinforcers**, or actions, can you add to them to make them more powerful? For example, *I'm going to stop and notice when something goes right and tell myself, "Nicely done!"* Be thoughtful of the messages you choose to reinforce.

For the limiting phrases, what are **countermeasures** you can take to reframe them to something more helpful? Ask yourself if you would tell a friend the things you tell yourself. If not, why? Insert what you would like to tell yourself instead.

RECAP

The top four ways to manage your voices to align your stars:

1. Use your Valuable Voice to help you adjust your mindset.
2. Notice what the Vicious Voice is telling you and counter it.
3. Know that how many friends you have on your sideline matters less than the friend that you have within yourself.
4. In Template 2, map the things you tell yourself that are both useful and limiting. Find ways to reinforce the useful things and counteract the limiting ones.

RESOURCES

- *Reboot: Leadership and the Art of Growing Up by Jerry Colonna*
- *The movie: Inside Out*

- *Who Owns the Ice House? Eight Life Lessons From an Unlikely Entrepreneur* by Gary G. Schoeniger and Clifton L. Taulbert

※ ※ ※

The right mindset helps you to start on the journey. Your mindset creates and builds momentum. Next, let's talk about how momentum is the key to your Execution Constellation to *Make Opportunity Happen.*

METHOD 3

The Magic of Momentum

"You don't have to be great to start, but you have to start to be great."
—ZIG ZIGLAR

I REMEMBER DAY ONE OF ORBIS. AT MY DESK IN MY SPARE bedroom, I asked myself, *Where do I start?* We didn't have a lab space, website, customers, revenue, or employees. It was exciting though. It was a blank page that we got to fill in. A few weeks later, the headlines said, "Lehman Bros meltdown shakes world's markets." Things just got real.

If you have felt the uncertainty, confusion, and overwhelm of, *Where do I start?* then you know what I'm talking about. Once you start, the path forms in front of you. Like the Martin Luther King Jr. quote, "You don't have to see the whole staircase, just the first step." You take that step. Then you see the next step, and you take that step.

Then you reach a place where you have three options for the next step. Creative as you may be, you cannot cram all the steps into one. You only have one opportunity for the next step. You can paralyze yourself by overanalyzing the right action. Run the experiment to get the data to tell you which way to go (see

Method 25). Trying something and learning the answer is often faster than overanalyzing.

There is the concept of thinking of decisions like "one-way" and "two-way" doors. One-way doors are decisions that, once made, give you one way to go. Two-way doors allow you to walk back into the room and choose again; you get a do-over if you don't like what is on the other side of the door. It's like building a house. Setting the foundation size is a one-way decision. The color of a room is a two-way decision as it isn't as challenging to redo.

Decisions that are two-way doors mean that you can return and try again if it doesn't work out. You lose time, so the faster you get information to confirm or disprove the decision, the better. Find methods to test along the way if the action was the right one, but don't second guess yourself. Make a decision and move on.

Time is the biggest thing to protect in your Execution Constellation. The next thing you know, six months go by, then another six months. I left my corporate gig to go on an entrepreneurial adventure. It was a leap of faith right before the market crashed in 2008. Listening to the bleak news later that year, I thought, *Wow, I am so lucky. Had I not jumped when I did, it would have been another five years before I would have felt comfortable leaping. By then, kids would be in the picture so that I would have never felt comfortable.* There is never a perfect time to take the entrepreneurial plunge. Sometimes, you have to say, "Today is the day!"

There is never a perfect time, nor is any idea perfect from the start. The magic of momentum is it's the juice that gets the next thing moving. It's important because it makes everything after it come so much more easily.

Your motto should be to *make the first step as easy as possible.*

This applies to the first step for you, your customer, investor, employee, or whoever you want to take action. Make the first step as easy as possible, and it gets easier to take the following steps.

To make things easier for yourself:

Focus and get in the zone. Use environmental aspects like music and location. When you put on your focus playlist (e.g., "The Theory of Everything" soundtrack), you focus and get it done. You are in creative brainstorming mode when you put on your energy playlist (e.g., Spotify's "Getting HYPED"). When you sit on your couch, you brainstorm product ideas. When you go to the coffee shop, you put details on those ideas.

Get the uglies out of the way. The uglies are things you don't want to do, but you need to do them. Sometimes, unpleasant things rot with time because we let them hang over our heads. Rip the Band-Aid and get the uglies out of the way.

Get things going. The first hour of my morning is a routine that fuels my mind, body, and soul. I give myself an hour of meditation and exercise. Later, when I sit at my desk and look at my to-dos for the day, I cross off my morning power hour. Include a few critical, quick items at the beginning of the day to get momentum before you get into longer, more demanding activities.

Stay in the moment. There is a Netflix Headspace video on mindfulness where cars move across the screen. You see the cars come and go, and you let the cars pass. You don't stay fixated on the cars, allowing them to spin out before you. Similarly, with your ideas moving through your mind, have a pad of paper next to your computer so you can capture those ideas and focus on what you are doing.

Try ten quick things. Look at the whole thing that needs to get done. Then, start with *ten little things* like responding to ten emails, following up on ten sales deals, or putting ten things away in your office. You lose track of time; the next thing you know, your inbox is empty, your sales follow-up is done, or your office is clean.

Get to the first draft. Start chipping away at the task; the magical momentum shows you what to do next. Don't worry about the final version. Just get to the first draft.

Help future you. Leave yourself an easy jumping-off point to restart the work tomorrow or the next time you pick it up. Put a sticky note with the first three things you will do when you pick up the project. Make it easy to start next time. Save yourself the *Where was I?* energy to get momentum going quickly.

Template 3 maps how to get from where you are to where you want to be. Brainstorm the list of actions. Don't judge the list or think about how hard the tasks will be. Just write them down. After you think you have about 80 percent of the actions, rank them on a scale of one to ten with ten being the most important. Next, consider which steps you can bucket together—marketing, funding, strategy, or operations—and see if there are themes. Write down who you can delegate something to. If it's just you at this stage, write down from whom you will seek guidance. Next, put an order on the list to start to give it structure.

I have a friend who has notebooks full of these lists and couldn't function without them. It helps with stress because you have so much to do at once. If you get it down on paper, your mind doesn't have to work hard trying to keep track of all the ideas in your head. The ideas in your head need a place to go. And as you start to write, other thoughts come. Paper is excellent because it's fast and disposable, so it doesn't need to be perfect. Besides having a drink in your hand, there's a reason many good things start from the back-of-the-napkin drawing.

Another trick is to plan the top three things you want to do each day, and at the end of the day, write down the top three things to start the next day. This helps automatically launch you into those actions rather than needing to figure out what to do next.

Momentum is the key to forward progress. Think about the easiest first step and then the easiest next step. Once you start in motion, it's easier to stay in motion.

THE *magic* OF MOMENTUM

(3)

I am here: _____   I am going: _____

| ACTIONS | PRIORITY | BUCKET | WHO | RESOURCES | ORDER |

I will be here by the end of the week: _____

MONDAY	TUESDAY	WEDNESDAY	THURSDAY	FRIDAY
Start here:	**Start here:**	**Start here:**	**Start here:**	**Start here:**
1.	1.	1.	1.	1.
2.	2.	2.	2.	2.
3.	3.	3.	3.	3.

Template Notes

You can download a printable version of this template at: makeopportunityhappen.com/templates/03

At the top of the template, write down **where you are** and **where you're going**.

In the **actions** column, brainstorm the things you need to do to get from here to there. Don't evaluate–just write them down. In the **priority** column, rate the importance of this action on a scale of 1–10. In the **bucket** column, ask yourself if the actions fall into certain categories or "buckets." In the **who** column, write down who will accomplish the action or who will help you accomplish it. In the **resources** column, list what you'll need to accomplish the action.

Lastly, plan where you'll be at the **end of this week** by listing three things you can do to get started. Make your first step as easy as possible and give yourself clear instructions.

RECAP

The top four ways to use magical momentum to align your stars:

1. Make the first step as easy as possible by focusing and getting in the zone, changing your environment to suit a specific action, and getting the uglies out of the way.
2. Get things going by staying in the moment, doing ten quick things, and getting to the first draft.
3. Help the future you by listing the next three actions to tackle.
4. Map out where you are and where you want to go in Template 3. Brainstorm the steps, resources, and priorities along the way.

RESOURCES

- Startup Reading https://startup-reading.com/
- *Atomic Habits: An Easy & Proven Way to Build Good Habits & Break Bad Ones* by James Clear
- *The Power of Habit: Why We Do What We Do in Life and Business* by Charles Duhigg, Mike Chamberlain, et al.
- *The Miracle Morning: The Not-So-Obvious Secret Guaranteed to Transform Your Life (Before 8AM)* by Hal Elrod

❋ ❋ ❋

Starting is half the battle in your Execution Constellation. After you start, make sure you are clear about where you want to go. Everything builds from this vision. Let's look into that next.

METHOD 4

Knowing Where You Want to Go

"If you don't know where you're going, you'll end up someplace else."
—YOGI BERRA

I AM A BELIEVER IN NEW YEAR'S DAY RITUALS. WHERE DO you want to be at the end of the year? How are you going to get there? In business, I start thinking in December, so it's not a snap decision on January 1. Inevitably, there are adjustments as the year progresses, but you know the direction you are going.

Ask entrepreneurs where they want to be in a year, and you can tell the entrepreneurs who have thought about it and let it guide their actions and decisions and the ones who haven't. The entrepreneurs who have thought about it have clear, specific, articulate plans. These entrepreneurs inspire confidence in their teams, customers, partners, and investors. The entrepreneurs who haven't specifically planned out where they will be in a year are flying by the seat of their pants, hoping it will all work out and not making progress.

In your Execution Constellation, knowing where you want to go means having clear, concise goals that you think about often and let guide your actions. You have measurements in place to track your progress. Your team knows and understands these three to five goals. Knowing where you are going helps you progress toward the goal, keeps your team engaged, and lets you sleep better at night. This is key in your Execution Constellation.

Get clear on where you want to be in twelve months, and break your tasks and goals into quarters. Then, break the first quarter into three months and the first month into four weeks. These are the building blocks to where you want to be in a year.

Compare your goals for the next thirty days to those you set for the end of the year. How do they match? Does achieving your goals in the next thirty days help you reach the end-of-the-year goal? Often, you ignore the end-of-the-year goal, and the thirty-day goals have nothing to do with the end-of-the-year goals. If you keep doing this, how will you make the end-of-the-year goals? Do you think you'll get a year's worth of goals done in month twelve? Often, it's a sales metric where you have this problem. Selling is scary. Selling is where it all gets real.

If the actions that are needed to get to your annual goals don't show up anywhere in the first month, restructure your thirty-day goals so that it's a building block to the larger goals. If sales are the primary driver, but only one person has 10 percent of their work effort dedicated to sales, that is a problem. Put a spotlight on it and figure out how to rebalance near-term goals to ensure your thirty-day actions set you up to achieve your one-year goals.

For your team's individual goals, plan for your company first and translate it to each team member. For all your goals, it's essential to be clear on the result so everyone knows if you achieve it. Make sure the goal is measurable, specific, clear, and has a deadline.

It's a bad deal if someone on your team is calling it a win when you don't hit the milestone the goal intended to achieve.

An example could be, *Get three clients.* You think this implies that these clients are paying your company. If your team onboards three non-paying clients, they may be ready to break open the bubbly. You will wonder how you will pay their salaries. Get specific and clear on all goals so that everyone understands what the metric means.

In setting individual team members' goals, make sure:

- You align individual and team goals.
- Individual goals are reasonable, doable, and provide the right level of motivation.
- Individual goals are specific to the person.

People are more engaged in their goals when they have input on how the individual goals come together. Give employees the team goals and show where they fit into them. Work with individual team members to determine the right individual goals. If people set their goals too low, refer to the company goals and ask them to work with you to align their individual goals to achieve the team goals.

Develop safety buffers in your goals. If you need three paying clients, set individual goals for four or five clients. This gives you room to make sure you get three clients.

Communicate clearly and in advance, so people have time to work toward their goals. No one likes the goalpost moved on them. People want clear communication of where the goalpost is and how much time they have to work toward it. Don't give them their annual goals in September if the deadline is December.

In the company's early stages, you are learning so fast that things are changing quickly and specific goals can become irrelevant. One way to address this is to leave some flex in the goals.

Getting *$500k in revenue* is better than selling *100 Superturbos*. It provides flexibility if you need to adjust midyear when you realize the market wants Turbosupers instead of Superturbos. You may need to replace obsolete goals. Remember that you will need to remain fair *and* take goals seriously to keep your team engaged.

In communication, it's good to be transparent about everyone's goals. It brings comfort to know where the company is going and who has what part of the goals covered. Everyone wants to know how each other's goals fit together to create the whole. This also helps with team cohesion, a sense of belonging, and peer accountability. Everyone wants to see how they fit into the team's goals, and no one likes disappointing other team members. Remember to celebrate wins as a team.

KNOWING *where* YOU WANT TO GO

④

ANNUAL GOALS

1.
2.
3.

QUARTER 1 GOALS
1.
2.
3.

QUARTER 2 GOALS
1.
2.
3.

QUARTER 3 GOALS
1.
2.
3.

QUARTER 4 GOALS
1.
2.
3.

MONTH 1 GOALS
1.
2.
3.

MONTH 2 GOALS
1.
2.
3.

MONTH 3 GOALS
1.
2.
3.

WEEK 1 GOALS
1.
2.
3.

WEEK 2 GOALS
1.
2.
3.

WEEK 3 GOALS
1.
2.
3.

WEEK 4 GOALS
1.
2.
3.

Template Notes

You can download a printable version of this template at: makeopportunityhappen.com/templates/04

For your company, break down your **annual goals** into **quarterly goals**, your first quarter into **monthly goals**, and your next month into **weekly goals**.

Repeat the same template for each team member where your individual team member goals reflect the overall company goals, and get specific on what metrics track each goal.

RECAP

The top four ways that knowing where you want to go helps align your stars:

1. Have three to five clear, concise goals you think about often that guide your actions and measure your progress.
2. Use Template 4 to establish where you want to be in twelve months and break your goals into quarters, months, and weeks to establish building blocks. Compare your near-term and annual goals to ensure alignment. Complete these goals annually and update them monthly.
3. Translate team goals into individual goals. Make sure individual goals are reasonable, doable, motivational, and specific to the person.
4. Document and share goals and tracking with your team so everyone is on the same page.

RESOURCES

- *Rework* by Jason Fried, David Heinemeier Hansson, and the *Rework* podcast
- Founder Library: https://www.founderlibrary.com/
- How to Start a Startup—A course Y Combinator taught at Stanford: ycombinator.com/library/carousel/How%20to%20Start%20a%20Startup%20-%20A%20course%20Y%20Combinator%20taught%20at%20Stanford
- Y Combinator Library: https://www.ycombinator.com/library

❋ ❋ ❋

A repeatable, simple process of setting goals for your team as a group and as individuals helps everyone know what they need to do. Now that you know where you are headed, make sure you are working on the right things to move your stars in your Execution Constellation.

METHOD 5

The Right Things Right Now

"Work on the things that matter, not just the things that are urgent."
—STEPHEN COVEY

I HAVE WORKED WITH DOZENS OF ENTREPRENEURS ON SETting and tracking their Key Performance Indicators (KPIs). A KPI is:

> A quantifiable measure of performance over time for a specific objective. KPIs provide targets for teams to shoot for, milestones to gauge progress, and insights that help people across the organization make better decisions.[2]

Working with entrepreneurs, we focus on metrics in ninety-day sprints and have weekly meetings to discuss their progress. With the roller coaster of the entrepreneur's life, it's easy to come to the weekly KPI meetings saying, "Now, what is my KPI again?" The many hats you wear can be overwhelming, and distractions make it challenging to progress toward a goal.

---

[2] "What Is a KPI?," Qlik, accessed November 7, 2023, https://www.qlik.com/us/kpi.

To understand why this is such a problem, look at another way experts talk about a KPI:

> What's the most important thing we have to achieve as a business right now? Why does that thing matter? How will you know you've achieved it?[3]

So, your KPI is *the most important thing to do*—yet, you *can't* remember what it is!?! Not focusing on the most important thing is a significant reason you do not progress. Further, KPIs apply beyond the common "revenue" or "conversion rate" metrics. Don't assume KPIs apply only to revenue-generating companies; you'd miss the opportunity to use them to drive your growth.

In your Execution Constellation, dig deep to determine if your chosen KPI is *the most* important thing and if you chose the right way to measure it. Metrics evolve, so KPIs are not set in stone, but make sure you change the metric for the right reasons. If you have the right KPI but are failing at making progress, figure out how to make progress on the KPI rather than changing it.

Next, consider how you break your work effort toward that KPI into specific action items. What are the experiments you need to run? What obstacles are in your way? Once you have the insight, it should be about the discipline required to execute.

While KPIs focus on the most important thing, during a company's early stage, it can be too difficult to set just one KPI. There are multiple things you need to do. A top-three approach

---

[3] Amos Schwartzfarb and Trever Boehm, *Levers: The Framework for Building Repeatability into Your Business* (Carson City, NV: Lioncrest Publishing, 2021).

may be better for you as many things are critical to the company's success. This format may look like this:

- **Revenue:** increase monthly recurring revenue to $50k
- **Team:** hire the Chief Technology Officer
- **Funding:** secure a $500k convertible note to provide a cash runway

When I hired a key scientist, I said, "This is our top priority!" and "This is our top priority!" and "This is our top priority!" I joked about it at the time, but our reality was that we had several important priorities. You may find yourself where, as discerning as you can be, you still have three to five *top* priorities. If this is you, you are in good company, as Einstein often worked on multiple theories simultaneously. He could have a breakthrough on Light Quanta or Brownian Motion while letting the Theory of Relativity marinate.

Success in a startup is about having enough balls in the air that you have something to work with when one ball drops and not too many things that it jeopardizes something getting across the finish line. This is a critical path to navigate. It's a dance between having a bigger vision that people want to come along with you and a laser focus so you can make progress toward that bigger vision. It's important to avoid getting a case of *Shiny Object Syndrome* when you get distracted by anything *shiny* that comes your way.

So, how do you know if you are in the right place on the Goldilocks spectrum of enough things going on but not too many? Here is a series of questions to help you decide if you are where you should be:

- How many of these do I need to meet my goals? How many

sales calls do I need to get to my ideal number of sales? How many proposals do I need to get the customers I need?
- How do I make these things easy and efficient while maintaining quality? How do I use templates, automation, delegation, and recycling of other work?
- What do I do if this client goes away along with the revenue? Do I have other avenues to keep going? What percentage of my business suffers? How do I mitigate that?
- How do I scale beyond this stage? Are there partnerships that can help me do that? What do I need to prove to get there?
- What would happen if I completely stopped doing this activity? If it's "not much," and I can't see that changing anytime soon, I should stop doing that activity now.

When in doubt, do the things that will make you money today. Keeping the lights on is usually priority number one; it buys you time to get to your other priorities.

Your KPI measures the most important thing your business needs to achieve. Get it right and focus on it; you are in much better shape to get where you want to go.

THE *right things* RIGHT NOW

(5)

KPI	MEASURED BY			
	HOW	WHO	WHEN	SHARED WITH

KPI EXAMPLES

SALES:
- Number of New Contracts Signed Per Period
- Dollar Value for New Contracts Signed Per Period
- Number of Engaged Qualified Leads in Sales Funnel
- Net Sales (Dollar or Percentage Growth)

CUSTOMER:
- Number of Customers Retained
- Percentage of Market Share
- Net Promotor Score
- Average Ticket/Support Resolution Time

OPERATIONAL:
- Order Fulfillment Time
- Time to Market
- Employee Satisfaction Rating
- Employee Churn Rate

MARKETING:
- Monthly Website Traffic
- Number of Qualified Leads
- Conversion Rate for Call-to-Action Content

FINANCIAL:
- Revenue Growth
- Net Profit Margin
- Gross Profit Margin
- Operational Cash Flow
- Current Accounts Receivables
- Inventory Turnover
- EBITDA

Template Notes

You can download a printable version of this template at: makeopportunityhappen.com/templates/05

To determine your **KPIs**, ask yourself: *What is the most important thing we need to achieve as a business right now?* How will you know when you've achieved it?

Then, determine **how** you will measure your KPI, **who** will measure it, **when** they measure it, and who the information will be **shared with**.

RECAP

The top four ways to work on the right things to align your stars:

1. Go deep on evaluating your KPI. Ensure it's your number one priority that you need to achieve as a business right now. Check that you pick the right way to measure progress toward your goal.
2. Use a top three KPI approach when you have many needs that seem to be *the most important thing*.
3. Talk yourself through the questions to pressure test your KPIs.
4. Define your KPIs in Template 5 to detail how you measure and share your KPI information.

RESOURCES

- Techstars Entrepreneur's Toolkit: https://toolkit.techstars.com/
- Startup Hacks by Alex Iskold: https://www.startuphacks.vc/

- *Levers: The Framework for Building Repeatability into Your Business* by Amos Schwartzfarb and Trevor Boehm
- *Measure What Matters: OKRs: The Simple Idea that Drives 10x Growth* by John Doerr
- *Do What Matters Most: Lead with a Vision, Manage with a Plan, Prioritize Your Time* by Rob Shallenberger and Steve Shallenberger
- *Smarter Faster Better: The Secrets of Being Productive in Life and Business* by Charles Duhigg, Mike Chamberlain, et al.

❋ ❋ ❋

Once you have a good handle on the right KPIs and measurement system, rethink what you are working on today to see how it ties in with your KPIs. This helps you shed what isn't helping you and gives you a laser focus on what is working in your Execution Constellation.

METHOD 6

What to Work on Today

> "If you can't fly then run, if you can't run then walk, if you can't walk then crawl, but whatever you do you have to keep moving forward."
> —MARTIN LUTHER KING JR.

IN MY FIRST JOB OUT OF COLLEGE, MY COMMUTE INCLUDED four lanes, with 90 percent of us in the right lane waiting to get on the highway for miles before we needed to be in that lane. I learned to stay in the left lane. When I got closer to the highway entrance ramp, I waited my turn to merge. This kept me moving forward rather than sitting three stoplights back.

I remembered this learning in my early days at Orbis. I would focus on one *stoplight* at a time and tell myself, *My only job right now is to get through this stoplight.* Yes, you have a vision of the entire way home, but you don't have to get bogged down on what is down the road when the immediate need is to get through this traffic light. In the startup world, chunk it into each traffic light. Break the entire path into bites, then focus on one bite at a time.

When you plan your path to align your stars in your Execution Constellation, take a sheet of paper and write where your goal is and the steps you need to take to get there. Use this set of questions and get as specific and granular as you can:

- What do I need to do to get across this finish line?
- Look at each item on the list and ask, *What do I need to get these things done?*
- Repeat these questions until the items on the list are small so you can do them individually.

Focusing on the immediate goal reduces your stress and lets you make better decisions. When you are so focused on being in the right lane two miles away, you don't realize you could get through this light in the left lane. Merge when the other cars have stopped at the last light.

The other trick I took in staging work was thinking in parallel rather than linearly. When starting a company, you think, *I will raise funding, get customers, be wildly successful, and sell the company!* You will get stuck somewhere (it's usually funding) and stop making progress. This is thinking in a series. A better method is to think in parallel.

Parallel thinking separates the items so they aren't dependent on each other, and you can make progress on each separate pathway. Do X *while doing* Y *while doing* Z. So by breaking those things into their specific workstream, you get:

- Raise funding → Define your opportunity → Identify potential funders → Develop your presentation → Get introductions → Start the process
- Get customers → Define the pipeline → Determine how you reach your customers → Draft your messaging → Experiment to find evidence that customers want what you are selling

- Be wildly successful → Determine your team structure → Find potential employees → Build a great team
- Sell the company → Make a list of target buyers → Get introductions → Start to get to know potential buyers

You get many paths to the finish line when you operate in parallel. If you get stuck in one place, the other lines' paths can continue to make progress. Progress on one pathway (e.g., customer traction) helps you make progress in other ways (e.g., fundraising). If you are stuck waiting for something to come together, ask yourself, *What can I start on the other pathway now while I'm waiting on this item?*

It's all about having options and making progress. You may get stuck at one point (fundraising) but make significant progress on another path (getting customers). You can wake up one day and realize you do not need to raise as much funding as you thought or that you don't have a suitable business model, and it does not matter how much money you raise. Either way, working in parallel helps you get there faster.

In Template 6, list your top five goals and the top ten bite-sized actions that will move you forward on your goals. The last column, "For You," lists how you care for yourself. We often forget this part. It's that "put your face mask on first when the plane goes down" thing. You can't do everything you need to do if you aren't getting enough oxygen yourself.

Break larger goals into bite-size goals to make it easier to get things moving. Break goals into many paths so you can make progress in some if you get stuck in other areas.

WHAT TO *work on* TODAY

GOAL 1	GOAL 2	GOAL 3	GOAL 4	GOAL 5	FOR YOU!

1.

2.

3.

4.

5.

6.

7.

8.

9.

10.

Template Notes

You can download a printable version of this template at: makeopportunityhappen.com/templates/06

Ask yourself these questions to break down your big **goals** into manageable chunks.

- *What bite-sized tasks can you break it down into?*
- *Can you break things into multiple parallel paths?* This will make it easier to get things going and keep making progress on some paths even if you get stuck on others.
- *What goals are just for you?* Renew yourself while you're making progress on your goals. Write them down in the **for you** column.

RECAP

The top four ways to rethink what to work on now to align your stars:

1. Know the entire path home and then focus on getting through the next traffic light.
2. Break things into parallel paths so you are making progress even if you get stuck somewhere on another path.
3. List your top five goals and the top ten bite-sized actions that will move you forward on your goals in Template 6.
4. Make sure you have action items *for you* to give yourself enough oxygen.

RESOURCES

- *The E-Myth Revisited: Why Most Small Businesses Don't Work and What to Do About It* by Michael E. Gerber

- Y Combinator Library: https://www.ycombinator.com/library
- *The Personal MBA* 10th Anniversary Edition by Josh Kaufman

※ ※ ※

Knowing what you are working on helps you think about where to go next in your Execution Constellation. One of the best ways to align your stars is to establish a culture of accountability. Accountability starts with you and then extends to your team.

METHOD 7

Accountability for You and Your Team

"Accountability is the glue that ties commitment to the result."
—BOB PROCTOR

GROWING UP ON A FARM, YOU LEARN ACCOUNTABILITY AT a young age. One of my dad's favorite sayings is, "If it's to be, it's up to me." He somehow incorporated this motto into our DNA. It's one thing for you to have the accountability gene. It's different when establishing it in your team. The first method seems simple: pick people on your rocket ship with the accountability gene too. Sometimes, it's difficult to see at first, but it's something to test for and see in action. One litmus test is to watch their words: do they take responsibility for things that didn't go well or do they blame others?

Accountability is accepting responsibility and the consequences of your actions and decisions. Often, it's other people who hold us accountable by saying, "How is that coming along? Whatever happened to that? Did you get your homework done?"

But when you are an entrepreneur, you need to hold yourself accountable. It's not only "Did you get it done?" but also "Did you get it done in a way that will keep your company alive?" "In a way" relates to your resources with time and money being the biggest. The question becomes, "Did you get it done quickly enough?"

Accountability is essential because it moves you forward to your goals, helps you make decisions, and creates an environment where other accountable people want to be. Those are the people you want on your rocket ship.

In your Execution Constellation, consider accountability in three buckets: you, your team, and your clients and partners. These buckets follow a scale from the most to the least control. All of these parts need to move with you to make progress.

Track your ability to get things done with the following two questions:

1. What is your system?
2. What is your discipline?

Do you have an intentional system and revisit it to make improvements, or do you let it all just happen to you? Do you have the discipline to stick with your system? When things break down, look at both parts to determine what to fine-tune.

Communication is one of the most significant needs for a working system, particularly email. I leveraged my inbox as a to-do list for many years, and while I was successful, it was draining. It wasn't until I got to inbox 0 that I realized how freeing it is.

Everyone has their system; just make sure it's intentional. Make sure you own it, and the system doesn't own you.

One of my favorite things is my Friday to-do list:

- Weekly Plan
    - Revisit my mission and goals
    - Decide the top three goals for next week

- Plan for next week
- Time block the important steps for my top three goals
- Clean the office and organize notes
- Get to inbox 0
- Go through my follow-up list

This weekly practice helped me focus on the most important things to make progress.

There are other helpful practices like team meetings. The secret of team meetings is that it not only helps your team deliver but also helps *you* deliver. The most helpful meeting structure we found was to cover the top three goals for the week, results from the top three goals from last week, and any challenges. This structure helps you focus and answer the question: *What are my top three goals?* This motivates you to follow up on those top three goals because you must report on them next week.

Chunking the goals makes it straightforward if you did it or not. *I will post the job description and interview five candidates* is better than *I will work on hiring a salesperson*, and *I am going to get introductions to the top ten investors on my target list* is better than *I am going to fundraise*. It should be clear whether you can cross each goal off the list at the end of the week.

These are often called SMART goals: Specific, Measurable, Achievable, Relevant, and Time-Bound. It's an easy checklist to see if you missed something. Who wants a goal that is irrelevant or not achievable, right?

When you want to get something done, put it out there for others to see. Your top three list at team meetings is great for this. Give it a dedicated focus on your to-do list and calendar.

Have a system and discipline on how you and your team get things done to increase accountability.

accountability FOR YOU AND YOUR TEAM

ACCOUNTABILITY CHART: YOUR TOP THREE GOALS

	WEEK 1	WEEK 2	WEEK 3	WEEK 4	WEEK 5	WEEK 6
PLAN	1.	1.	1.	1.	1.	1.
	2.	2.	2.	2.	2.	2.
	3.	3.	3.	3.	3.	3.
RESULT	1.	1.	1.	1.	1.	1.
	2.	2.	2.	2.	2.	2.
	3.	3.	3.	3.	3.	3.
LESSONS	1.	1.	1.	1.	1.	1.
	2.	2.	2.	2.	2.	2.
	3.	3.	3.	3.	3.	3.

Template Notes

You can download a printable version of this template at:
makeopportunityhappen.com/templates/07

Use this accountability chart for you and each member of your team. In your chart, write down your top three **goals** at the beginning of the week. At the end of the week, write down the **result** of each goal and keep track of any **lessons** you learned. For example, "I tend to be over-optimistic on sales goals" or "I don't allow enough time to perform team development goals."

Create a chart for each member of your team, following the same process, and help them identify **trends** and **solutions** to any problems.

RECAP

The top four ways to use accountability to align your stars:

1. Use accountability to move you toward your goals, help you make decisions, and create an environment where other accountable people want to be.
2. Consider accountability in three buckets: you, your team, and your clients and partners.
3. Have a system and discipline in your accountability. When things break down, look at both parts to fine-tune. Use Template 7 to document your top three weekly goals.
4. Leverage tools like your weekly plan and team meetings to help you focus and make progress rather than progress.

RESOURCES

- *Traction: Get a Grip on Your Business* by Gino Wickman
- *Crucial Accountability, Second Edition: Tools for Resolving Vio-*

lated Expectations, Broken Commitments, and Bad Behavior* by Kerry Patterson
- *Profit First: Transform Your Business from a Cash-Eating Monster to a Money-Making Machine* by Mike Michalowicz

✻ ✻ ✻

Accountability with you and your team is the best place to start. Then, focus on increasing accountability with your clients and partners. These skills are key in your Execution Constellation, so get good at it.

METHOD 8

Accountability for Your Clients and Partners

"The greatest leader is not necessarily the one who does the greatest things. He is the one that gets the people to do the greatest things."
—RONALD REAGAN

THERE WAS A SALES OPPORTUNITY I HAD BEEN NURTURING, and nurturing, and nurturing. Most people told me to move on, saying, "Your time is better spent somewhere else." One Saturday morning, the client finally emailed, saying, "You are very patient and persistent. We are going to go forward with the project." I can still remember the EUREKA moment when I got that email!

Clients and partners are critical to your mission. Clients buy your product and services, and partners help you offer your product and services to your clients. Clients buy; you don't sell to them. Partners choose to work with you; you can't make them work with you. It takes a certain level of savviness to make progress with your clients and partners when they have lots of freedom to walk away.

Following the golden rule is key to getting clients and partners to move forward in the Execution Constellation. Treating others the way they want to be treated applies to clients and partners through:

- **Alignment.** What is in it for them? Know their pain points and provide a solution to their pain. Create alignment between what they need and what you have.
- **Momentum.** Make it as easy as possible for your client to work with you. If you want to move things along, do as much of their work as possible for them. Can you draft it for them? Can you send an email they can forward to introduce you to their procurement team? Can you make it easy for them to decide? Get creative on how you can make your desired outcome easier for them.
- **Autonomy.** When moving something forward, ask your client for the timeframe for the next step. Often, it's, "I will get that to you in a week," which seems reasonable at the time. But a week comes and goes quickly. People are more motivated to put it on the top of the list when they have missed a deadline they set for themselves rather than the one you set for them.
- **Ease.** Don't overload them with options or ask them what they want. Sometimes, you think you are a good partner by exhibiting so much flexibility, but really, you make it harder for them to decide among many options. Listen to what they need and give them a prescription, or narrow their choices to A and B. Even when setting up a time to talk next, giving them two options makes it easier for them to say yes or no. Saying, "What time next week works for you?" gives them a bigger job. Research shows too many options keep us from moving forward. Make it easy for them to decide.

Besides the importance of the problem you are solving for the client, good communication is your best tool to move things forward. These are a few things that help:

- **Use concise emails.** When emails are too long, it's too much work to get through them.
- **Send the email to one person.** If you send it to a group, you risk the person thinking someone else should respond or take action. Sometimes, this means sending three emails to three different people. That small time investment is worth it.
- **Follow-up.** When people get too many items in their inbox and need to prioritize, they will think, *Let's see if they follow up. If it's important to them, they will check in and ask how it's going. If they don't follow up, I assume it was not that important.* Follow up and let them know it's important.
- **Follow a friendly escalation plan.** The number of people who just sit and wait for the email reply is incredible. We've had experiences where our contact left their company, and we wondered why they weren't responding to our email. It's because they aren't there anymore! Find a new contact at the company!

For your friendly escalation plan, consider: (1) email, (2) follow-up email, (3) call, and (4) check in with a peer if you don't hear anything back with a genuine and polite question: *Is everything OK?* Not with a *Why aren't they getting back to me?* If they are on their honeymoon and didn't tell you, filling their inbox with many messages won't make them happy when they return.

The friendly escalation plan is all within a well-thought-out timeframe. You don't do all four steps in twenty-four hours.

Having a regular progression that you follow makes it an automatic routine, so you don't let yourself sit around waiting for an email reply.

If it's something super important, Step 5 includes showing up at their office with a smile and a plan for helping them get it done quickly.

It's important to have options for clients and partners. It takes two to tango, and if you find the relationship is too one-sided or too much work, find another dance partner. It's easier to shift partners when you have already spotted other dance partners, and they are eager to get on the dance floor.

Generating accountability for your clients and partners includes bringing a set of golden rules to help you increase accountability.

accountability (8)
FOR YOUR CLIENTS AND PARTNERS

I ACHIEVE ALIGNMENT BY:

I GENERATE MOMENTUM BY:

I PROVIDE AUTONOMY BY:

I MAKE IT EASY BY:

MY COMMUNICATION APPROACH IS:

MY FOLLOW-UP STRATEGY IS:

MY ESCALATION PLAN IS:

Template Notes

You can download a printable version of this template at: makeopportunityhappen.com/templates/08

Complete the **statements** to define your go-to methods and develop your plan for achieving client accountability. Then incorporate your plan into your **best practices** and workflows and refer to it when you get stuck or need to find a way to get things moving forward.

RECAP

The top four ways to generate accountability with your clients and partners to align your stars:

1. Follow the golden rule to get clients and partners to move forward. Treat others the way they want to be treated.
2. Use these ways to do this include:
   A. **Alignment.** Find what is in it for them.
   B. **Momentum.** Make it as easy as possible for your client.
   C. **Autonomy.** Ask your client for the timeframe for the next step.
   D. **Ease.** Simplify your client's options.
3. Follow good communication practices, including being concise, sending the message to one person, following up, and using a friendly escalation plan.
4. Plan your accountability methods in Template 8 so they become automatic.

RESOURCES

- *Disciplined Entrepreneurship Workbook* by Bill Aulet

- *Way of the Wolf: Straight Line Selling: Master the Art of Persuasion, Influence, and Success* by Jordan Belfort

※ ※ ※

One of the essential things in working with clients and partners is to find ways to increase their urgency. Urgency alignment is important in your Execution Constellation. This is how you can make progress at a pace that is a win for everyone.

METHOD 9

Urgency Builders

"Time kills all deals."

—ABOUT FIFTY PEOPLE I KNOW

YOU KNOW THE SITUATION. YOUR FRIEND SAYS, "I'LL BE here _____ (fill in the blank with any goal) in six months." The six months come and go, and the goal continues to slide, and slide, and slide. This is the perpetual "in six months" problem. We do this and then wake up realizing we have been talking about that goal for a long time.

There is a difference between accountability and urgency. Accountability is when you do what you say you are going to do. You are dependable. Urgency is when you have the proper speed to get it done. You have a fire within you. You need to deliver both accountability and urgency in the Execution Constellation.

When selling our company, people advised me, "Time kills all deals!" I would reply, "I know! I know! What more can I do?" It's like the dot-com bubble burst of 2000, where you had the IPO of your dreams before March 10, 2000, or you faced bankruptcy after March 10. Eventually, something will change in the world that will kill your deal.

As luck would have it, as we approached the finish line in selling Orbis, a pandemic hit! During this time, I told myself that if I were to write a book, the title would be *Urgency*. Thinking about the company's history, there was often a mismatch between our urgency and the other party's urgency. We often brainstormed different ways to create urgency, calling these *Urgency Builders*.

Having a culture of urgency helps you attract folks who want to get stuff done and appreciate urgency. When you have this mindset, it's easier to *Make Opportunity Happen*.

These are some of my favorite Urgency Builders for creating movement with yourself or your team. I used many of these in writing this book.

- **Start the clock.** Commit to finishing X in seven days or Y in thirty days.
- **Put a date on the calendar.** Set the presentation date, meet with a potential customer, or travel to the conference.
- **Tell someone about it.** Tell your friends or coworkers, announce it on LinkedIn, and just put it out there.
- **Get an accountability partner.** Make a bet with a friend and text daily. Tell an accountability peer group and report monthly.
- **Get an accountability coach or mentor.** Meet weekly with someone who will motivate you to achieve your goals.
- **Spend money.** Buy the plane ticket or pay the graphic designer.
- **Fill out the application.** Apply for TEDx, or Global Entrepreneurship Week, in this book's case.
- **Have board or advisor meetings.** Set the meetings with the purpose of making progress toward company goals.
- **Update investors and stakeholders monthly or quarterly.**

Motivate yourself and your team to report certain things by the next written update.
- **Get coconspirators.** Line up a product or marketing person to help you.
- **Help the virtual assistant help you.** When someone needs you to figure out your part before they can do their part, you must get it done. You don't want to waste their time.
- **File a provisional patent.** If you invent intellectual capital in the form of patents, file the provisional patent, put a stake in the ground, talk about it, and start the clock. You have twelve months to complete the details. That $3k to $5k patent cost has value as an urgency builder, perhaps even more than the patent itself.

The above strategies help you move toward your goals. Use them to get momentum going or get you unstuck.

Sometimes, you are in the middle of the day-to-day grind, and an urgency builder isn't going to help you. At those times, here are several ways to think about this:

- Know your priorities and values.
- Ask yourself every day what you can do to advance those items.
- Plan it out by breaking it down into bite-sized chunks.
- Write it down, complete the task, and cross it off.

These four steps build clarity and direction. Crossing things off your list gives you the boost to keep going.

When thinking about creating urgency in others, think about momentum. When you are in motion, you tend to stay in motion. When people start taking step after step, it's easier just to keep walking than to stop and decide to go in another direction.

When working to build urgency for others, try these strategies:

- **Make it as easy as possible for your customer to take the first step.** You don't need them to buy your product or service today. Can you start by getting a ten-minute call on their calendar?
- **Build momentum steps.** When you get to A, then B happens, then C happens, etc. Each step is easy and builds on the last step.
- **Find ways to save them time.** From small things like making it easy to read your email to big things like making the case they can use with their boss.
- **Put a deadline on it.** Let your client or partner set the date. Ask them for a reasonable target date when wrapping up the conversation.
- **Have a respectful check-in reminder.** Let them know it's important and ask if you can help them.
- **Bring it to the top of the list.** Focus on their pain and how it gets worse if they don't act. Take steps to solve their pain.
- **Ensure the other party has skin in the game.** Don't do free work. Your customer needs to pay or have a handshake agreement of where this is going should the initial steps be successful. Confirm handshake agreements by email within twenty-four hours or, better yet, in an official agreement.
- **Leverage that everyone hates late fees.** Define late fees in payments at the beginning of the relationship when everything is going great in case you need to refer to the policy later.
- **Appeal to their sense of fairness and pride in their reputation.** If it's a situation they wouldn't want their boss to know, that creates an incentive to take action.

- **Introduce the fear of missing out.** When all else fails, remember that the risk of missing an opportunity can be highly motivating. Loss aversion—the risk of loss—is a powerful urgency builder. Just remember that you may have to go away. There isn't a *just kidding* button to push with this urgency builder.

Avoid the urgency killers of overwhelming, annoying, or angering your client. Don't make it hard for them or require a lot of their time. That is when it's easy to have an external force disrupt the momentum and tell them, "Go in a different direction."

To create urgency to avoid the perpetual "in six months" problem, use Urgency Builders that help you, your team, and your clients get things done.

urgency BUILDERS

FOR YOU:

- [ ] 1. START THE CLOCK _____
- [ ] 2. PUT IT ON THE CALENDAR _____
- [ ] 3. TELL SOMEONE ABOUT IT _____
- [ ] 4. FIND A FRIEND OR GROUP _____
- [ ] 5. USE A COACH OR MENTOR _____
- [ ] 6. SPEND MONEY _____
- [ ] 7. FILL OUT THE APPLICATION _____
- [ ] 8. HAVE THE BOARD MEETINGS _____
- [ ] 9. UPDATE STAKEHOLDERS _____
- [ ] 10. GET COCONSPIRATORS _____
- [ ] 11. HELP THE VA HELP YOU _____
- [ ] 12. FILE A PROVISIONAL PATENT _____

FOR OTHERS:

- [ ] 1. MAKE THE FIRST STEP EASY _____
- [ ] 2. OBTAIN MOMENTUM _____
- [ ] 3. SAVE THEM TIME _____
- [ ] 4. ASK THEM TO PUT A DEADLINE ON IT _____
- [ ] 5. HAVE A GOOD FOLLOW-UP GAME _____
- [ ] 6. HELP THEM BRING IT TO THE TOP _____
- [ ] 7. REQUIRE SKIN IN THE GAME _____
- [ ] 8. INCLUDE LATE FEES IN PAYMENT TERMS _____
- [ ] 9. APPEAL TO THEIR SENSE OF FAIRNESS _____
- [ ] 10. CONSTRUCT THE POSSIBILITY OF LOSS _____

Template Notes

You can download a printable version of this template at: makeopportunityhappen.com/templates/09

Consider the list of **urgency drivers** for **yourself**. Check the methods that work for your goals and write down a plan for how you will accomplish them. Then repeat the process **for others**. Revisit the list when you're stuck and need help moving forward.

RECAP

The top four ways to create urgency to align your stars:

1. Know there is a difference between accountability and urgency. Accountability is when you do what you say you are going to do. You are dependable. Urgency is when you have the proper speed to get it done. You have a fire within you.
2. Chunk your goals into the appropriate sizes so they are doable and build momentum.
3. Use Template 9 as a checklist of urgency drivers, prioritize the methods, and refer to the list when you are stuck.
4. Avoid urgency killers, including overwhelming, annoying, or angering your clients, making it hard for them or requiring a lot of time.

RESOURCES

- "Inside the Mind of a Master Procrastinator," a TED Talk by Tim Urban
- "The Single Biggest Reason Why Startups Succeed," a TED Talk by Bill Gross

- "Get Comfortable with Being Uncomfortable," a TED Talk by Luvvie Ajayi

※ ※ ※

Urgency alignment is such an important skill in positioning your stars that you will want to get better at it continually. Let's close your Execution Constellation by addressing empowered decisions. You make many decisions throughout your venture. Have a framework to help you make good, quick decisions.

METHOD 10

Empowered Decisions

"You cannot make progress without making decisions."

—JIM ROHN

A KEY MENTOR TOLD ME THAT MY ABILITY TO MAKE DECIsions impressed him. I relished this comment as he had watched me make hundreds of decisions. Hearing his comment made me stop and think about how I made decisions. You get better and better at making decisions the more you do it. A decision-making structure also helps.

What do good decisions look like? You have the right level of information, data, and input to guide your decisions. You don't decide too quickly as that leads to rash decisions, and who wants a rash anyway? You don't decide too slowly as you get bogged down and lose people, time, and energy. Making good decisions matters because it gets you where you want to go.

Here is the five-step framework for how to make good, quick decisions in your Execution Constellation:

1. Use guiding principles
2. Know your nonnegotiables
3. Gather information

4. Communicate effectively
5. Move forward

The First Step: Use Guiding Principles. People who make *good*, quick decisions typically have a decision-making framework to help them quickly assess the situation.

I learned the concept of *guiding principles* early in my career. Whenever you embark on something new, get clear on your guiding principles. Post the principles where you can see them, and look at them when making decisions. It keeps you rooted in what is important and where you are going. When establishing your guiding principles, these are the questions to ask yourself:

- *What is important to you and your company?*
- *What are your values?*
- *What are your nonnegotiables?*

Getting clear on these three things is important for you and your company. When you know it, codify it in your guiding principles. This gives you a filter to screen options and make decisions.

I included a few examples.

Google's ten things we know to be true are:

1. Focus on the user, and all else will follow.
2. It's best to do one thing really, really well.
3. Fast is better than slow.
4. Democracy on the web works.
5. You don't need to be at your desk to need an answer.
6. You can make money without doing evil.
7. There's always more information out there.
8. The need for information crosses all borders.

9. You can be serious without a suit.
10. Great just isn't good enough.

Virgin Airlines lists their core values as:

- We think customer.
- We lead the way.
- We do the right thing.
- We are determined to deliver.
- Together, we make the difference.

The Second Step: Know Your Nonnegotiables. Knowing your nonnegotiables is crucial. You have to know them and walk away when needed. Walking away is super tricky to do. When you walk away, you often earn the most crucial form of respect: from yourself and your team.

This reminds me of my friend, Mike, who showed his team how much he valued them. One day, a customer came into their office and verbally abused one of his team members. Mike approached the customer, told him they don't talk like that here, and referred the customer to a competitor down the street. He invited the abusive customer *not to be their customer anymore*. He could do this because he clearly understood what was important to him (respecting his team) and his nonnegotiable was verbal abuse. When he experienced the problem, he could quickly decide what to do. After this day, Mike's employees had a deep respect for Mike and loyalty to his company. This became one of the company's defining stories.

The Third Step: Gather Information. In the example with the crappy customer, Mike needed to decide how to respond immediately. Many of your big decisions offer you more time to think about it. For example, you shouldn't make an impulsive decision to start your business. You gather information. There is a Goldilocks zone in the right amount of information: not too little or too much.

Rely on experts with specific knowledge about your business and the industry. You don't want just anyone's perspective. You want people who have done it before or have an important perspective on your situation. It's amazing how many people give advice on raising money and selling companies who have never done either themselves.

If they have been in your shoes a few times—even better. One of my board members had great success in picking an investment banker. He had researched investment bankers and had shared his insights with me. One of life's great tricks is having friends who do deep research and will share it with you. In return, be the friend who does deep research on some things and shares that with others.

Have a core of three to five people to bounce ideas off. Mine were knowledgeable on the subject and had valuable diversity of thought. Specifically, diversity in risk tolerance is helpful. A spectrum of risk tolerance from very protective to very opportunistic allows you to take their perspectives, weigh the pros and cons, and decide where you want to be on the risk spectrum. In startups, risks are inevitable. Risk insulation in certain instances is crucial as well.

If your brain trust's thinking lines up, this process also helps bring people along with you, especially if they are key stakeholders in the business.

Besides your counsel of advisors, gather information on success rates, time commitment, and strategies to assess an opportunity. In evaluating solutions to a problem, consider options, costs, risks, pros, cons, and timing. Pull this information together so you can see it. Often, the decision becomes obvious.

The Fourth Step: Communicate Effectively. Communication of decisions is important. Make sure everyone has the information and rationale behind your decisions. Your team wants to know you listened to their perspectives. They also take comfort in knowing the decision has been made, and they can plan how to move forward. Your team loses faith if you take too long to make decisions by getting mired down in too much information.

The Fifth Step: Move Forward. After you make the decision, *move forward*. Don't second-guess yourself. Don't go back and keep thinking about it. Sure, you should always look for new information. If you decide today and two weeks later, you have new information, consider that and make adjustments where needed. Always give yourself the option to make adjustments. But don't drive yourself or your team crazy waffling back and forth in decisions. Make a decision and move on.

If you do make decisions that DID turn out to be inarguably wrong, ask yourself these questions:

- *What do I learn from this experience?*
- *Where do I go from here?*
- *How do I adjust guiding principles to help me in future situations?*

In making decisions, it's helpful to have guiding principles of what is important to you and a decision-making strategy that you can use to make good, quick decisions.

EMPOWERED *decisions*

(10)

MY DECISION: _____

MY GUIDING PRINCIPLES:	DOES IT MEET MY GUIDING PRINCIPLE?
	☐
	☐
	☐
	☐
	☐
	☐

Template Notes

You can download a printable version of this template at: makeopportunityhappen.com/templates/10

Create your **guiding principles** so that you can filter your **decisions** through them. Ask yourself: *What is important to me? What are my values? What are my nonnegotiables?* These are the sources of your guiding principles.

Your guiding principles stay constant, and the questions that require decisions change.

When considering if your decision **meets your guiding principles** or not, ask yourself, *Would doing this bring me closer to this value/objective?* If so, your guiding principles and your decision are in alignment. If not, your decision doesn't meet your guiding principles. If you don't know, how can you try it out to help you decide?

RECAP

The top four ways to empower your decisions to align your stars.

1. Have the right information and input to guide your decisions.
2. Use the five-step framework to make quick decisions using guiding principles, nonnegotiables, information, communication, and moving forward.
3. Develop guiding principles in Template 10 that help you quickly screen decisions with criteria that are important to you.
4. Look for new information, and when it arises, consider making adjustments.

RESOURCES

- *Thinking Fast and Slow* by Daniel Kahneman, Patrick Egan, et al.
- "The Art of Choosing," a TED Talk by Sheena Iyengar

※ ※ ※

Making good decisions is key to aligning your stars in your Execution Constellation. As you journey into your Support Constellation, you will learn that support is both within and outside you. You must manage your overwhelm, so let's talk about strategies to help you.

PART 2

Support Constellation

"If you want to go fast, go alone. If you want to go far, go together."
—AFRICAN PROVERB

YOUR SUPPORT CONSTELLATION IS YOUR INTERNAL MINDSET and the people around you who form the structure to align your stars. No one does anything important alone. You need the people, insight, and backing around you to make it easier and to make the journey worthwhile.

The mindset methods are to manage your overwhelm and have methods to survive the entrepreneur's roller coaster. The key to your support is outfitting your rocket ship, understanding the founder and co-founder roles, a working framework, and providing Clarity of Structure to everyone on your rocket ship. You want to establish your culture code in your The Way We Work document. Understand hiring basics, the importance of your board, and Friendshelp, which is friendship crossed with help that creates the ultimate rocket fuel. These are the key elements of your Support Constellation.

METHOD II

Managing Overwhelm

"Stress is not what happens to us. It's our response to what happens. And response is something we can choose."

—MAUREEN KILLORA

A FEW YEARS INTO MY ORBIS JOURNEY, I HAD THREE-MONTH-old and three-year-old boys, and a good night's sleep was elusive. One of our key leaders turned in his resignation with two hours' notice. After he delivered the news, I needed to meet with a consultant. As I walked down the hall to the meeting, an employee stopped me in his panic, saying, "Did you hear he just quit? What are we going to do?"

We proceeded through the consultant meeting like it was business as usual. The consultant didn't know about our internal turmoil. Then, out of the blue, the consultant told a story about managing people, and he said, "And that is why I stopped hiring people. I got tired of training them, and they left as soon as they could do something." I thought, *That is too poetic.* I said to the consultant, "I hear you." We walked out of the meeting and figured out what to do next.

Our team had two big grant proposals with a looming deadline. Our technical leader and I decided what changes we could make to the grant proposals in the time we had. When I think of being overwhelmed, I think of this story mainly because I wondered if I would sleep through the night ever again.

Do you sometimes feel you have so much to do like you will die or at least fall over? When entrepreneurs are in their trusted circles, one of the most common words you hear is *overwhelmed*. So, if you feel overwhelmed, you are not alone.

Stress is when these things are hard, but you will persevere and complete them. Overwhelm is when there are too many things coming at you at once. You can't process them all, much less deal with them. Overwhelm is the feeling when everything seems like it's too much. You are anxious and stressed about everything you have to do. You try to do too much simultaneously, and the challenges seem insurmountable.

Overwhelm decreases productivity and causes burnout, health problems, and relationship damage. You get paralyzed about what to do next, and your mind spirals down and goes into the "Should I be doing this?" zone. Managing overwhelm is crucial for your mental and physical health and the ability to align your stars in your Support Constellation.

The best guard against overwhelm is to take one thing at a time and to be present in the moment. Then, the fear of the future or the regret of the past does not seep in. There is only the current moment. You prioritize, solve problems, and sift through minutiae to get to what matters and is realistically doable. I used to have my days full of meetings and traveling. Then, at 5:30 p.m., I would look at my to-do list and see two days' worth of tasks to complete *that day*. I would say to myself, *What was I thinking?*

When it comes to overwhelm and burnout, sometimes there is a disconnect between expectations and reality. The disconnect is often about timing and how quickly you expect results.

An optimistic outlook is important, or else you will never start. Realistic expectations are important so you don't overcommit, lose faith, or set yourself up for problems.

There is a joke that entrepreneurs "have to be crazy to do this." The data shows that entrepreneurship is negatively correlated with mental health. The reasons are stress, uncertainty, social isolation, lack of access to mental health resources, and a predisposition to mental health challenges. Two other reasons include: (1) *impression management* of needing to *have it all together* and not showing weakness and (2) having your identity and self-worth fused with your company.[4]

Your emotions are a chemical response to your thoughts. You don't recognize the thought before the feeling, so your chemistry can make you uncomfortable quickly. A tool that Dr. Susan Anderson created is: "I feel _____ because _____." This helps us connect the two sides of our brain to put reins on our emotions. Our brains reconcile perceived problems. Unsolvable problems are at the heart of our discomfort.

Leaders provide certainty to ease the anxiety of those who work for them. The certainty is often confidence in the group's ability to handle difficult things. Creating an environment of certainty does not mean that emotions are dead. Dr. Daniel Goleman's book *Emotional Intelligence* focuses on using your emotional aptitudes to read people and situations, manage your backstory, and use emotions as fuel.

Other suggestions to manage overwhelm are prioritizing connection, noticing where expectations are out of line, making

---

[4] Megan Bruneau, "7 Reasons Entrepreneurs Are Particularly Vulnerable to Mental Health Challenges," Forbes, April 4, 2018, https://www.forbes.com/sites/meganbruneau/2018/04/04/8-reasons-entrepreneurs-are-particularly-vulnerable-to-mental-health-challenges/?sh=7022f64b63a3.

self-care nonnegotiable, working with a coach or therapist, finding other sources of self-worth and meaning, and redefining what success and failure mean to you.[5] It's important to learn how to show up for yourself during difficult times, using your Valuable Voices (Method 2), and to treat yourself like you would treat a friend.

When you enter the overwhelmed zone, give yourself a time audit and follow a three-step plan to manage your overwhelm.

Think of your time audit like a financial audit that reveals how you spend your time rather than your money. You need to understand where you are before you make changes. This helps you:

- **Understand** where you spend your time.
- **Prioritize** what you can cross off your list or move to the future.
- **Design** how you want to spend your time.
- **Crush** any negative thoughts.
- **Get help** from others to help you get past the overwhelm.

Here is a three-step plan for your time audit:

1. **Chart.** Look at your calendar and chart how much time you spend on internal meetings, client meetings, networking, email, planning, sales, funding, operations, projects, social media, water cooler, and industry knowledge.
2. **Visualize.** Now that you know the pie chart, envision what you think the pie chart should be. What is the right balance

---

5   Megan Bruneau, "7 Strategies Every Entrepreneur Should Employ to Optimize Their Mental Health," *Forbes*, April 7, 2018, https://www.forbes.com/sites/meganbruneau/2018/04/07/7-strategies-every-entrepreneur-should-employ-to-optimize-their-mental-health/?sh=2f17f6bd1fa7.

of things? What things shouldn't be on the chart or where should you do less (i.e., email)? What things should be on your pie chart that aren't yet (i.e., exercise)?
3. **Plan.** Ask yourself how you get from where you are to where you want to be. The first step is awareness. There are no magical wands to help you make the change immediately. If you don't need to do things (or at least not now), make those changes. Then, consider where you can delegate, automate, and restructure the pie chart.

It goes from:

- "I had no idea emails consumed 25 percent of my day" (understanding) to "I check email at 10:00 and 3:00" (prioritized and planned).
- "I have to squeeze in the 'time to think' when I'm on the toilet" to "I get great insights when I have time to think, and it's on my calendar."
- "Exercise took a back seat to everything else" to "Exercise is baked into my day, and it helps me do better on all my other work."

Do this weekly and then think about the time audit and pie chart restructuring in ninety-day and annual cycles. If you want to take fifteen days of vacation this year and don't see any days off on the ninety-day calendar, ask yourself if you should restructure. That is when you see how your actual vacation, time with family, and other important things stack up with your personal goals.

Beyond the restructuring, focus on what you can do *right now*. Prioritize effectively, and then make your immediate list to work on today. Order that list and start going down the list.

If it still feels overwhelming, break it down into the next hour and just focus your efforts there.

The first part of managing overwhelm is to give yourself a time audit. The next part is the three-step plan to manage your overwhelm.

MANAGING *overwhelm* (11)

WHERE I AM

WHERE I WANT TO BE

STEPS TO MOVE ME FROM WHERE I AM TO WHERE I WANT TO BE:

1. _____
2. _____
3. _____
4. _____
5. _____

Template Notes

You can download a printable version of this template at: makeopportunityhappen.com/templates/11

On the **top left chart**, think through how you spend your time. Put down the top five activities and estimate how much time you spend on each by looking at your calendar for the last few weeks or keeping track over the next few weeks. Then, think about how you would like this pie chart to look in the future. What is the optional time spent on these things? Is there something that should be in the top five but isn't? Sketch this in the **top right chart**.

After you consider how you spend your time and have a game plan for where you want to be, decide the **steps** you're going to take to get you there. Can you cross off some things? Can you delegate some tasks? Can you reset your expectations? How do you help yourself say no to things that won't get you closer to where you want to be?

RECAP

The top four ways to manage your overwhelm to align your stars:

1. Minimize overwhelm because it decreases productivity and motivation and causes burnout, health problems, and relationship damage.
2. Give yourself a time audit to see *how* you spend your time and how you *want* to spend your time.
3. Follow a three-step plan to manage your overwhelm:
    A. Look at your calendar and chart your time on specific tasks.
    B. Envision how you want your time allocated on your pie chart.

   c. Ask yourself how you get from where you are to where you want to be.
4. Use Template 11 as a framework to assess what you spend your time on and how you want to spend your time.

RESOURCES

- *Burnout: The Secret to Unlocking the Stress Cycle* by Emily Nagoski and Amelia Nagoski
- *Emotional Intelligence* by Barrett Whitener, Daniel Goleman, et al.

❄ ❄ ❄

Part of managing overwhelm is to have solid survival strategies for your roller-coaster ride. These strategies help you turbocharge your Support Constellation. Learning how to do this is so vital that it is explained in the next method.

METHOD 12

Roller-Coaster Survival

"Life is like a roller coaster. You can either scream every time there is a bump or you can throw your hands up and enjoy the ride."

—UNKNOWN

THE PHRASE "ROLLER COASTER" IS ONE OF THE MOST USED phrases in describing the entrepreneur's journey. One of my clients said, "Sometimes, it's going up, down, backward, and forward all at the same time."

A time when I felt this roller-coaster chaos was after signing a services agreement to work on an exciting product. The ink was dry on the contract. Our "Yes! Yes!" moment was quickly followed by a "No! No!" moment the next day when a woman from the partner's business development department demanded terms that we didn't give to any company. We had no choice but to end the contract.

We love the highs of the entrepreneur's ride and do what we can to minimize the lows. How do we manage the ups and downs? Let's address how to develop the steadiness muscle in an environment of many ups and downs. This is a key star in your Support Constellation.

There are climbs when everything is going in the right direction, and you think, *It's going to work! This is fun!* Then you are in free fall, and you move into, *It's never going to work! Get me off this ride!* When most of the scary stuff is worrying about the future, it's helpful to rethink how you handle your fears.

The first step is to identify the specific source of anxiety. Is it because you are procrastinating and making things worse than they are? Is it because you have taken on too much and must figure out how to get it all done? Is it because you've taken a healthy dose of rejection and must rebound? Is it because you worry about things beyond your control? As hard as you try, you can't make the other person sign the agreement, invest, or buy the product.

The following checklist helps you put things into perspective.

- What's the worst thing that will happen? If you can live with that, stop worrying.
- Will it matter in ten years? One year? One month? One week? If it doesn't matter in the future, stop worrying.
- What will you learn from it? If you are going to learn from it, there is always value, and it's worth doing.
- What are my values and priorities? Looking at what is important to you helps frame the immediate experience in a way that is meaningful or just doesn't matter.
- What is the bigger picture? Focusing on the larger goal helps you get through the real-time pain.
- How might someone else view this situation? Channel people you admire who can let things roll off their backs to see how they would view the situation.
- Is there another way to do this that is better? Sometimes, tweaking things changes how you experience them.

Pick your favorite questions to help you see situations from different angles. This helps you move through the experiences with a different attitude. Many people avoid directly thinking about failure. But sometimes, confronting the fear of failure and wondering, *What would life be like if I did fail?* is the best remedy because you realize that you will be able to move through it.

Additionally, make a plan for what you need to do today. Once you make your plan, quit living in the future and take the next step. Find evidence that helps guide your thinking. If you worry about failing but can point to plenty of times you have come through just fine, then lean into that. Refer to Method 21, with its menu of longer-term mindfulness habits to put you in a state to better enjoy the ride.

To survive the roller coaster, use questions to help you put things into perspective and enjoy the ride.

12
roller coaster SURVIVAL

FLOWCHART OF QUESTIONS TO HELP MANAGE THE ROLLER COASTER

WILL IT MATTER IN TEN YEARS? IN ONE YEAR?

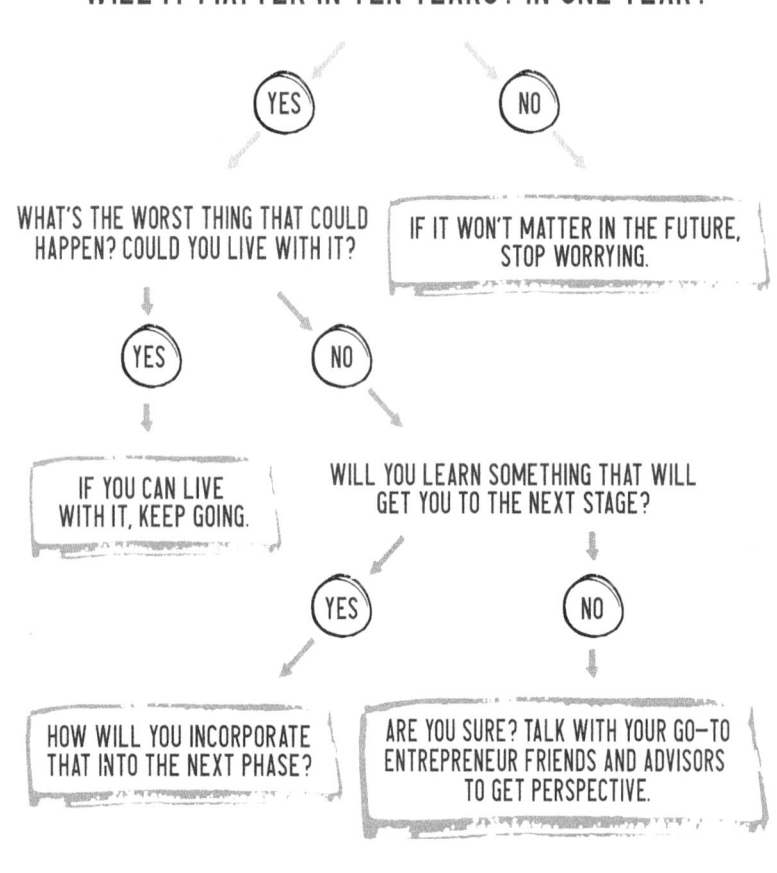

- **YES** → WHAT'S THE WORST THING THAT COULD HAPPEN? COULD YOU LIVE WITH IT?
  - **YES** → IF YOU CAN LIVE WITH IT, KEEP GOING.
  - **NO** → WILL YOU LEARN SOMETHING THAT WILL GET YOU TO THE NEXT STAGE?
    - **YES** → HOW WILL YOU INCORPORATE THAT INTO THE NEXT PHASE?
    - **NO** → ARE YOU SURE? TALK WITH YOUR GO-TO ENTREPRENEUR FRIENDS AND ADVISORS TO GET PERSPECTIVE.
- **NO** → IF IT WON'T MATTER IN THE FUTURE, STOP WORRYING.

> ## *Template Notes*
>
> You can download a printable version of this template at: makeopportunityhappen.com/templates/12
>
> For areas of stress or situations you're worried about, take your concerns through the **flow chart**. When you get to the end of the decision tree, ask yourself how you will **incorporate it** into your next phase. If you're sure you're not going to learn anything from it (which is highly unlikely!) talk it through with your go-to entrepreneur friends to get some perspective.

RECAP

The top four ways to survive the roller coaster to align your stars:

1. Find the ways to manage the ups and downs in the entrepreneur's roller-coaster journey.
2. Identify the specific source of anxiety and use the checklist to help you put things into perspective.
3. Focus on what you can do today.
4. Use Template 12 to help you think through specific turbulent points you encounter on the roller coaster.

RESOURCES

- *The EOS Life* by Gino Wickman, Steve Edwards, et al.
- *13 Things Mentally Strong People Don't Do: Take Back Your Power, Embrace Change, Face Your Fears, and Train Your Brain for Happiness and Success* by Amy Morin

✷ ✷ ✷

Perhaps the biggest star in your Support Constellation is your founding team, the core group of co-founders, leaders, and employees in your crew. You are assembling a team for your rocket ship. This early team is a vital part of your Support Constellation.

METHOD 13

Your Rocket Ship

> "It's not about getting more people on the rocket ship, it's about getting the right people."
>
> —UNKNOWN

WHEN I WORKED AT CERNER, I WAS IN THE RIGHT PLACE AT the right time and got to join the founding team of the next new thing. Neal Patterson, Cerner's CEO, leaned over and said, "This is like going on a rocket ship. There are only four seats. Who sits in those other three seats?" I thought of this conversation many times over my entrepreneurial journey.

A startup is a rocket ship. There are only a few seats on the ship. Who gets to sit in those seats? Whether in determining co-founders or the early employees, think strategically about who those early people are. You are going into uncharted territory. You need people beside you who can do many things, figure stuff out, and make it work. The only thing you know is that something on that ship will malfunction. Pick people you trust to fix the ship and get you safely home.

When assembling your team, you want common characteristics *and* diversity in skills and experience to align this star in your Support Constellation. For common characteristics, you need a shared mission and values. Everyone needs solid leadership, teamwork, and communication skills. Think deeply about the things that should be your common core. A good human factor and the ability to treat each other well were high on our list.

Because the company has limited seats, you need diversity in those seats. It doesn't matter that everyone can code if no one can sell. The skill sets on your list depend on your company type. For example, regulatory expertise matters if you are a pharmaceutical company, but it doesn't make your list if you have a tech product in an unregulated industry.

Here is how to think about your internal assessment. First, identify what you need to have in common. Leadership qualities? Check. Teamwork traits? Check. Communication abilities? Check. Next, think of diverse needs for a well-rounded team. Think about the core of the business and ensure that it's filling a seat on your ship. Technology companies do best with a technology founder on the team. If you outsource it, that's like outsourcing the engine of your rocket ship. Get the most important expertise on the ship before you launch if it's core to your business.

Here is a checklist of functions that you will want on your rocket ship:

- Leadership
- Research & Development
- Marketing & Sales
- Industry Experience
- Human Resources
- Finance & Accounting
- Operations & Supply Chain
- Customer Support & Service

- Legal & Compliance
- Quality Assurance & Testing

When you are a small team, you won't have a person dedicated to each area, but someone has to do it. Get outsourced help where needed. I wouldn't tell anyone to be their own lawyer. There are also things that people will do better and faster than you (e.g., your taxes). Think "best use of resources." If it takes you ten hours to an accountant's one hour, it's better to outsource your accounting.

Even if you outsource it, someone inside the organization should own it. Make sure you have a name next to each function so you aren't looking at each other thinking someone else is taking care of it.

Identify your "next key hire(s)." You may not have enough cash to hire these roles early, but knowing the next important hire is important. You can start to identify those individuals early so you can act when the time comes. Perhaps you will even get lucky in finding someone who values equity over salary.

Determining who is on your rocket ship helps you think strategically about assembling the early team. You want to think through common characteristics and diversity of experience and skill set you want on the ship.

YOUR *rocket ship*

(13)

CULTURE CODE + TRAITS I NEED:

COMMON CORE

VALUES:
_____
_____
_____
_____

GOALS:
_____
_____
_____
_____

ROLE SPECIFIC

EXPERTISE:
_____
_____
_____
_____

_____
_____
_____
_____

_____
_____
_____
_____

RESPONSIBILITIES:
_____
_____
_____
_____

_____
_____
_____
_____

_____
_____
_____
_____

Template Notes

You can download a printable version of this template at: makeopportunityhappen.com/templates/13

Define the **common core** among your values and what you want in a diverse set of skills. At the top of the page, write down the things that are important to have in common. What are your common goals? Do you need to be in the same location? It's better to know these things up front than to decide later that something is essential and not a common thread.

Then, write down your top three **roles** (for example, CEO, CTO, COO, etc.) in the blue boxes and their core functions on the lines. Who is covering what functions? Who is bringing what expertise? Who leads sales, raises money, has deep industry knowledge, develops the product, and is the visionary?

RECAP

The top four ways to determine who is on your rocket ship to align your stars:

1. Think strategically about each seat because there are only a few seats on your rocket ship in the beginning.
2. Know the common characteristics everyone should share, including your mission and values.
3. Consider where you need diversity. Think of diversity in functions, experience sets, backgrounds, networks, and points of view.
4. Use Template 13 to outline the areas needed and who has what covered.

RESOURCES

- *Extreme Ownership: How U.S. Navy SEALs Lead and Win* by Jocko Willink and Leif Babin
- *Leaders Eat Last: Why Some Teams Pull Together, and Others Don't* by Simon Sinek
- *Safe People: How to Find Relationships That Are Good for You and Avoid Those That Aren't* by Henry Cloud and John Townsend

✷ ✷ ✷

When you have the right people on your rocket ship, you need to make sure you've got the right leadership at the helm. Whether you go the solo founder or the co-founder route, there are important considerations in your Support Constellation. Bolstering yourself as a solo founder and collaborating as co-founders is a key star in *Making Opportunity Happen*.

METHOD 14

Founder and Co-founders

> "The co-founder relationship is like a marriage; it requires love, understanding, and commitment to make it work."
>
> —STEVE JOBS

SOME OF THE MOST HEARTBREAKING STORIES ARE THE co-founder breakups. The best-friend relationship ending with one co-founder showing up to work to find the locks changed and their next steps requiring lawyers. You can say, "That will never happen to me!" Then, I think of the solo founders who carry the weight of the world on their shoulders with no one to share it with.

Make a thoughtful decision about flying solo or finding a co-founder. If going the latter route, align co-founder expectations and a plan for how to work together.

If you listen to some investors, they'll tell you that most of their investments are in co-founder teams. Co-founders are more successful in raising money, with 55 percent of investments going to companies with co-founders. However, most companies that have successfully exited exit with a solo founder.[6]

---

6 Haje Jan Kamps, "Breaking a Myth: Data Shows You Don't Actually Need a Co-Founder," TechCrunch, August 26, 2016, https://techcrunch.com/2016/08/26/co-founders-optional.

If you are a solo founder, decide whether to continue flying solo or look for a co-founder. Consider this litmus test:

- What does your company need to be successful?
- Can you get funding on your own?
- Do you want to go it alone, or do you want to have a wingman or wingwoman?

The main priority is building a successful company and creating the team structure around it. A big part of a company's success is getting the resources to build the team. Whether through funding or early revenue, investors and customers like to see a team rather than a person. Having a co-founder-led team is a criterion for many investors. They may need to see a technical co-founder if you are a tech company. If you are a solo founder, ask yourself if you can get the funding to hire the founding team on your own. If not, a co-founder may help you get funding.

Going alone is lonely. Having someone to lean on and share the responsibility is worth a lot.

If, for any of the reasons above, you decide you need a co-founder, ask yourself:

- *Is this person's experience and knowledge critical, or can you hire a founding employee?*
- *How dedicated is this person? Will they leave once it gets hard and isn't fun anymore?*
- *How critical is this person to the business? What would happen if this person left?*

If the answer to the last question is "not much," then keep looking.

If you stay a solo founder, get a good support system around you. Skip the rest of this method and spend more time with Method 20, Friendshelp, and Method 18, Hiring Basics.

For my co-founder friends, let's discuss how you can set yourself up for success in the Support Constellation.

What do good co-founder relationships look like? It's somewhat akin to good marriages. There are important principles at the foundation of both co-founder and marriage relationships. It's about trust, good communication, shared vision and goals, collaboration, commitment, compromise, conflict resolution, and emotional support.

Why does a good co-founder relationship matter so much? A co-founder breakup is a top reason for company failure. On average, 10 percent of co-founders end their partnership within the first year, and another 45 percent end within four years.[7]

The main reasons for failed co-founder relationships are mismatched personalities and work styles, strategic disagreements, conflicts regarding compensation, and differences in the vision for the company.

To prevent these problems, the questions are:

- How do you get co-founder alignment?
- What are the things to consider when you start?
- How do you improve the relationship over time?

Set guidelines for what you think success looks like. There are many elements of what success is. A friend tells a story where he sat down with his executive team and said, "If our company is successful, but all of our marriages fail, that isn't

---

[7] Agnes Alpuero, "The Pain of Co-Founder Breakups: Do Startups Really Need Multiple Founders?," Vietcetera, accessed November 7, 2023, https://vietcetera.com/en/the-pain-of-co-founder-breakups-do-startups-really-need-multiple-founders.

success." Marital relationships usually aren't the first thing you think of when you sketch out goals for your company. But it shows there are many facets of what success means. Brainstorm all the elements of your success and then pick the ones that are most important to you.

Flesh out what each co-founder brings to the table now and in the future. Get specific. Often, a group of founders will get together, split the founders' stock shares equally, and have wildly divergent contributions and commitments. This dynamic sets you up for a co-founder breakup. Unequal work distribution combined with equal ownership is a ticket to resentment and dissatisfaction.

Provide for future changes. This is why stock-option vesting is so important. Vesting options over four years with a one-year cliff before vesting begins will provide for a couple of scenarios. In month ten, if one co-founder isn't pulling their weight, you can do something about it before they vest a large share of the company. If, at year two, someone gets sick, needs to take care of a family member, or decides their heart isn't in this anymore, they can stop vesting. People change over time. Things will come up, and not everything goes as planned. A vesting schedule helps with these challenges.

Put the terms into a legal agreement (see the Founders' Agreement Overview in Resources for a template). Include the terms of the co-founder relationship, equity ownership, vesting schedules, decision-making processes, and exit strategies.

Create a process for a standard way to review and give feedback. You can often trace relationship deterioration back to something small that went unaddressed and grew into a huge divide. Make time to regularly review the co-founder relationship. Provide constructive feedback and make necessary adjustments to strengthen the partnership.

In improving relationships over time, think about the structure and honesty you put into your communication. While there is no way to predict the future or how you or your co-founder will change over time, you can control how you communicate.

- **Use radical transparency.** If you feel something, say it. Withholding thoughts will cause more pain in the long run.
- **Share thoughts, but don't share decision-making power.** One person should always have the final decision-making power in their given domain to avoid arguments. For example, in sales, the CEO has final decision-making power. In tech, the CTO has final decision-making power. By having a single person who is in charge of a given domain, it helps make decisions quicker. Each co-founder listens to their other co-founder's opinions as they will want the same.
- **Get comfortable with disagreement.** When you disagree with your co-founder, it weighs on you. Co-founder relationships naturally have some underlying healthy tension. So, if you normalize that tension and think of it as preserving the company's health, it doesn't weigh so heavily.
- **Speak a bit of each other's language.** You don't want a "tech" person and a "business" person. You want a tech person who understands a bit of business and a business person who understands a bit of tech.
- **Have mutual respect.** Let everyone do their job. Everyone should feel like they can offer suggestions. Clarity of Structure (Method 15) helps define who has what covered.
- **Know yourself (and your co-founder).** Use tools like Culture Index in Resources to help you and your co-founder know how best to work together. If you can see how you best complement each other, you can set yourself up to reduce the friction.

Equity split among co-founders is often the first major test. It can have long-lasting implications for the business. Don't delay figuring out what working with your co-founders in difficult decisions is like. Consider these things when deciding what is a fair and equitable distribution:

- **Contribution.** Assess each founder's contribution in skills, experience, time, and financial investment.
- **Effort and time commitment.** Consider who is going full-time and how that gets rewarded.
- **Unique expertise.** Evaluate industry expertise, networks, investor connections, and other specialized skills.
- **Future responsibilities.** Consider how roles and responsibilities evolve in the future.

For co-founder relationships, set guidelines early on for what success looks like, have a regular way to review and give feedback, and carefully consider equity split.

COFOUNDERS
(14)

ALIGNED VISION AND VALUES

SHARED VISION

SHARED VALUES

WHAT EACH COFOUNDER BRINGS

COFOUNDER	SKILLS & EXPERTISE	ROLE & RESPONSIBILITY	SHARED WORKLOAD

HOW WE WORK TOGETHER

OPEN COMMUNICATION	CONFLICT RESOLUTION	FINANCIAL TRANSPARENCY	ADAPTABILITY

Template Notes

You can download a printable version of this template at: makeopportunityhappen.com/templates/14

In the first section, define your **shared vision** by asking, *What is your long-term goal for the company?* Define your **shared values** by asking, *What is most important to you?*

In the second section, write down what **skills** each co-founder brings to the company, as well as their **roles** and how they **share** or contribute to the company's success.

In the last section, write down what qualities contribute to **open communication** (i.e., how you share ideas, concerns, or feedback), **conflict resolution**, **financial transparency**, and **adaptability** (i.e., how you adjust strategy as the business evolves).

RECAP

The top four ways to set up co-founder relationships to align your stars.

1. Consider your company's needs when deciding to go the solo founder or co-founder route.
2. Set guidelines on what success looks like, allow for future changes, and have a solid communication structure.
3. Be thoughtful about co-founder equity split in the beginning because it's often a future point of friction.
4. Use Template 14 to establish an aligned vision and values, what each co-founder brings, and how you work together. This Clarity of Structure provides your team with the right information to increase accountability and autonomy.

RESOURCES

- Founders' Agreement Overview: https://www.law.upenn.edu/clinic/entrepreneurship/startupkit/founders-agreement.pdf
- Culture Index: cultureindex.com/
- *Crucial Conversations: Tools for Talking When Stakes are High* by Joseph Grenny, Kerry Patterson, et al.
- Startup Reading on Founding Team: https://startup-reading.com/best-startup-founding-teams

✳ ✳ ✳

Clarity of Structure starts with the co-founders. Everyone on your rocket ship needs to know the roles and responsibilities of each seat. *Clarity of Structure* is a powerful element of a well-functioning team. It is the star you will visit next in your Support Constellation.

METHOD 15

Clarity of Structure

> "Knowing your roles and responsibilities is like having a map to navigate the journey towards your goals."
>
> —JOHN C. MAXWELL

AT ONE POINT IN MY CAREER, THE CEO LOOKED AT MY COLleague and me and said, "You two, go do that." It was a big job, and we were both eager to show we were capable. We also knew this instruction was a recipe for disaster in stepping on each other's toes. Together, we needed to decide how to best move forward. I am proud that we had our egos in check and the ability to navigate who had what responsibilities. This was a great lesson in *Clarity of Structure*. Everyone wants to know what they are responsible for and where they fit. Everyone wants purpose, autonomy, and clarity.

Once your rocket ship is properly outfitted, it's important to have Clarity of Structure. This happens when everyone on your team knows where the team is going and they know how they fit into that plan. Everyone knows their responsibility and what everyone else handles.

It's like when you're playing baseball, and you know your position and where everyone else is on the field. When more than one player could catch a pop fly, someone has to "call" the ball. This prevents: (1) running into a teammate or (2) the ball from dropping between you. Clarity of Structure answers the question: *Who has what ball covered?* This structure is key in an aligned Support Constellation.

Providing information on who does what increases accountability and keeps people in their lane. Clarity of Structure *comforts* people because they know what they need to do and that everything else is being taken care of. Clarity *reduces frustration* because people don't step on each other's toes, with multiple people thinking it's their job. Clarity *reduces your risk* because everything is being taken care of by someone.

Create Clarity of Structure and list the roles and responsibilities (use Template 15). In an organizational chart, you see where everything fits. This prevents people from saying, "I thought that was *my* job!" and "Who has *that* covered?"

Check your lists in Template 15 to identify overlaps and gaps. The overlap is easiest to see, so clean up that first. Run different scenarios and see how it flows across the team and where handoff points are. Brainstorm what is missing and fill in the gaps. See where you lack handoffs and fill in the holes. Even teams already in progress benefit because the picture brings clarity and reveals where a person is overloaded.

Next, consider if everyone is in the right place. Assessment tools, like the Culture Index, are helpful in understanding yourself and others. When you know individuals' natural strengths and talents, you can compare them to the needs of the roles. You see where people match their roles well and where you should make adjustments.

Last, focus on communicating to make sure everyone has clarity. When your company is small, your entire team may take part in the process. Feedback, refinement, and getting buy-in are important. If your team is larger, now is the time to ensure everyone sees themselves on the chart, understands where they fit, and has a chance to ask questions. It's an evolving document, and sometimes you haven't considered some things.

As the company evolves, there will be balls coming from left field. The person who sees the ball first owns it until you can sit down and figure out who owns it permanently. Adjust the structure as new information comes up or new people join the team.

Remember to check in. When your organization is new, a more frequent check-in process, such as monthly, helps get feedback on what is working. As your company gets used to the Clarity of Structure, quarterly, biannual, or annual checks will ensure ongoing Clarity of Structure.

Providing Clarity of Structure defines who does what. This clarity gives your team the right information to increase accountability and autonomy.

CLARITY OF *structure*

(15)

CEO

1.
2.
3.
4.
5.
6.
7.
8.
9.
10.

1.	1.	1.
2.	2.	2.
3.	3.	3.
4.	4.	4.
5.	5.	5.
6.	6.	6.
7.	7.	7.
8.	8.	8.
9.	9.	9.
10.	10.	10.

Template Notes

You can download a printable version of this template at: makeopportunityhappen.com/templates/15

Complete the template to answer the question of **"Who does what"** for your company. List the **roles** at the top of each box and list the **responsibilities** of that person below. Notice where there might be imbalances in the responsibility loads of the team.

RECAP

The top four ways provide Clarity of Structure to align your stars:

1. Ensure Clarity of Structure when everyone on your team knows where the team is going and how they fit into that plan.
2. Confirm every team member knows their responsibility and the responsibilities of each other person on the team. Use Template 15 to document your structure.
3. Create your Clarity of Structure by:
    A. Listing the roles and responsibilities
    B. Identifying gaps and overlap
    C. Communicating to make sure everyone is on the same page
4. Check in to ensure the structure's clarity is working and make adjustments as needed. Businesses are highly evolving structures.

RESOURCES

- *Traction: Get a Grip on Your Business* by Gino Wickman
- *Who Not How: The Formula to Achieve Bigger Goals Through Accelerating Teamwork* by Dan Sullivan, Dr. Benjamin Hardy, et al.
- *Drive: The Surprising Truth About What Motivates Us* by Daniel H. Pink and his TED Talk

❋ ❋ ❋

In addition to Clarity of Structure, having foundational principles for team beliefs and how to treat each other is important. Treating people how they want to be treated is the bedrock of how to operate. This star in your Support Constellation becomes your true North Star.

METHOD 16

Culture Cornerstone

"Do unto others as you would have them do unto you."
—JESUS CHRIST

"Treat others the way you want to be treated."
—CONFUCIUS

"One should treat others as one would like others to treat oneself."
—BUDDHA

"What you wish upon others, you wish upon yourself."
—NAVAJO PROVERB

"I said it because that is what I would want others to say to me. I was following the golden rule."
—REMY FLYNN, AGE SEVEN

TREATING PEOPLE HOW THEY WANT TO BE TREATED HAS BEEN a beacon for me. It's most useful at times of extreme stress or uncertainty: when you need to have a crucial conversation, let someone go, fire a client, or call off a negotiation. At these painful times, I ask myself how I would want to be treated, and the next step becomes clearer.

I remember two negotiations where we were just too far apart, and I didn't think we would get to a place that worked for both companies. I didn't want to waste their time, and I didn't have time to waste. Thinking about how I wanted to be treated, I called them and was up front about the situation. I gave rationale and was considerate. One time, the companies parted ways and continued a friendly relationship. Another time, the partner found a way to better align with our terms.

There is magic in the golden rule. The golden rule as a cornerstone of your culture sets you up to win employees, clients, and partners. *Treating people the way they want to be treated* is simple to say. It can be difficult to put into action. It's like any habit: the more you do it, the easier it is to keep doing it. The golden rule determines the way you listen to people, speak to them, think of their needs, take care of things, treat them, see them, and remember them. How you treat others matters because it fulfills some of our basic human needs.

From an employee perspective, *treating people the way they want to be treated* matters when:

- Designing compensation packages that help employees fulfill their needs
- Providing transparency so team members can see and hear what is real, so they won't be surprised or blindsided
- Welcoming and affirming that employees belong at your company
- Listening to employee perspectives and incorporating their feedback
- Providing opportunities for employees to fulfill their potential and help them find meaning and purpose in their work

When communicating difficult messages, think of the phrase *candor and kindness*. You can be as direct as a sword, but that is often not helpful. To be direct, using candor with kindness is something to aim for.

Ask yourself: *How would **you** want to hear this?* And then, *How would **they** want to hear this?* The first question gets you most of the way there because you put yourself in their shoes. The second question clarifies what is right for *that* person, as we all have differences. Don't say it with a hug if you are working with a non-hugger.

Other questions to ask include:

- *What makes him comfortable?*
- *What makes her see this is the appropriate way?*
- *What pain do they have?*
- *How do you help them get rid of that pain?*
- *What makes him feel important?*
- *What motivates her?*

Transparency and respect are important. That is what you want in your leaders. Alignment and trust are important. That is what you want in your team. Incorporating *treat others the way they want to be treated* into your culture achieves transparency, respect, and alignment.

Using the golden rule as your culture's cornerstone provides a solid environment.

culture CORNERSTONE
TREAT PEOPLE THE WAY THEY WANT TO BE TREATED

HOW DO I WANT TO BE TREATED?
_____
_____
_____
_____

HOW DO I TREAT PEOPLE THIS WAY?
_____
_____
_____
_____

HOW DO I NOT WANT TO BE TREATED?
_____
_____
_____
_____

HOW CAN I AVOID TREATING PEOPLE THIS WAY?
_____
_____
_____
_____

HOW WILL I INTEGRATE THIS INTO MY CULTURE?
_____
_____
_____
_____

Template Notes

You can download a printable version of this template at: makeopportunityhappen.com/templates/16

Distill what *treat people the way they want to be treated* means to you and how you operationalize it. First, write out **how you want to be treated**. Think about communication styles, transparency, working styles, etc. Next, reflect on **the ways you treat people**. Think about how you **don't want to be treated**. What are the steps you can take to **avoid treating people this way**? Lastly, consider how you will **integrate** these things into your culture.

RECAP

The top four ways to set up a culture to align your stars:

1. Use the golden rule, *treat people how they want to be treated*, as a cornerstone of your culture which sets you up to win clients and the people game.
2. Remember that how you treat people includes listening to them, thinking of their needs, taking care of them, seeing them, and remembering them.
3. Outline what it means to incorporate the golden rule into your core principles. Write down how you want to be treated and the converse: how you don't want to be treated. Include the steps you take to do both.
4. Use Template 16 to distill what *treat people the way they want to be treated* means to you and how you operationalize it.

RESOURCES

- *Dare to Lead: Brave Work. Tough Conversations. Whole Hearts* by Brené Brown and her podcast
- *Radical Candor: Fully Revised & Updated Edition: Be a Kick-Ass Boss Without Losing Your Humanity* by Kim Scott, Teri Schnaubelt, et al.
- *The Culture Code: The Secrets of Highly Successful Groups* by Daniel Coyle

✶ ✶ ✶

Part of treating people how they want to be treated is ensuring they have what they need. As we evolved at Orbis, a useful tool was creating *The Way We Work*. I'd like to share that with you now so you can use it as a star in your Support Constellation.

METHOD 17

The Way We Work

"Alone, we can do so little; together, we can do so much."
—HELEN KELLER

IT'S USUALLY WHEN SOMETHING BREAKS THAT YOU REALIZE that you need more structure today than you had yesterday. One entrepreneur called me, saying, "She thinks that whenever it snows, she doesn't need to come to work. This is the kind of job you have to be here to do. The rest of us can find a snow shovel. What am I supposed to do?" I asked what her employee handbook said about work expectations. She didn't have a handbook and asked for an example.

At Orbis, we eventually evolved our employee handbook into what we called *The Way We Work*. One great thing about starting a company is you get to set the culture. You bring in the things you want to bring. You leave out the parts you don't want in. When you start, the culture may be loosely defined by the founders. You have principles or mantras that you repeat. You have beliefs of what actions are appropriate and out of bounds.

When you start your company, there are so many things to do and a lot of things to prove. Does your product work? Do customers want your product? What is the right price? How do you get customers? How do you get employees? You often have so much to do that sitting down and documenting how you work is not at the top of the list. It doesn't matter how great your company culture is if you don't have a company, right?

As you make more progress, you realize this thing called culture is SUPER important, and maybe you should do something about it. But how do you work on culture? One important thing we found was to write down our culture code in The Way We Work.

The Way We Work had the standard employee handbook items, and the most meaningful page was the first page that answered the question: *What do we stand for?* We defined how we would treat each other and how to make the company a great place to work. We included expectations for the treatment of associates, clients, and partners; a results-oriented environment; the communication code; and meetings, calendars, and work schedules.

This process codifies your culture. You do more than post it on your wall. You refer to it often and reflect on it. It can be aspirational, but the important thing is that you are actively working toward living the words on the page. The Way We Work backfires if the words are hollow and your actions don't match the words.

Draft your The Way We Work. Then, get feedback from your team. Once your team is big enough or as your team grows, bring in a consultant to survey if The Way We Work still holds true to your culture. Find action items that strengthen your culture alignment to The Way We Work. This helps with team buy-in and gives the words more meaning.

Our consultant surveyed us to see how well The Way We Work reflected our company and buy-in to these principles. For each key principle, our consultant asked us where we scored ourselves and our team. We graded ourselves on statements like: "I treat others with respect and enable others through encouragement and mentoring," and "You believe our company treats others with respect and enables others through encouragement and mentoring."

We looked at the words in The Way We Work and asked, "Why is this important?" And, "What is my contribution?" We went deep on asking, "Why?" five times to dig to the root of why we do what we do. Then we went through the actual words and asked, "Is that true?" And, "Are there better words?" We made tweaks to The Way We Work based on our results and refined the document as we learned more and our team grew.

Get clarity when an employee is not a good fit for your company by asking yourself, *Why was this person not a fit? What qualities, traits, or mindsets did the employee have or not have that you needed?* This mitigates hiring the wrong person in the future by including recruiting screening questions that address these cultural aspects.

The Way We Work codifies what is important to your culture. Keep it as a living document that evolves with you. Don't let it just be something you post on a wall. Make The Way We Work something that truly reflects who you are. This defines your culture so everyone understands how you do things as individuals and as a team.

THE WAY *we work* (17)

ASSIGNED / TEAM

_____
_____
_____
_____

CLIENTS / CUSTOMERS

_____
_____
_____
_____

ENVIRONMENT

_____
_____
_____
_____

COMMUNICATION

_____
_____
_____
_____

CALENDARS, MEETINGS, WORK SCHEDULES

_____
_____
_____
_____

Template Notes

You can download a printable version of this template at: makeopportunityhappen.com/templates/17

Capture the way you work by focusing on the important principles in each category. Ask yourself, *What is **important** to you and what is **appropriate** for the way you work?* Ask your team the same question to get their perspectives. Post your **The Way We Work** where you can see it and refer to it often. Keep it as a living document, evolving as your company evolves.

RECAP

The top four ways to establish The Way We Work to align your stars:

1. Set the culture. Bring in the things you want to bring and leave out the parts you don't want. Be intentional about what you bring and what you do not.
2. Codify your culture in The Way We Work and answer the question: *What do we stand for?* Use it to define how you would like to treat each other and how to make your company a great place to work.
3. Use Template 17 to decide the important points for the team, including customers, environment, communication, calendars, meetings, and work schedules.
4. Test The Way We Work to strengthen its alignment with your culture.

RESOURCES

- How to Write an Employee Handbook and What to Include in It: https://www.uschamber.com/co/run/human-resources/how-to-write-employee-handbook
- 7 Employee Handbook Examples You Should Steal From: https://www.zenefits.com/workest/employee-handbook-examples/
- *The Five Dysfunctions of a Team: A Leadership Fable* by Patrick Lencioni, Charles Stransky
- *Overcoming the Five Dysfunctions of a Team: A Field Guide for Leaders, Managers, and Facilitators* by Patrick Lencioni

❉ ❉ ❉

The key to establishing The Way We Work is having good hiring practices. Hiring basics is the next star in your Support Constellation.

METHOD 18

Hiring Basics

"Great vision without great people is irrelevant. Hire amazing individuals and give them the freedom to work their magic."

—ANITA RODDICK

I HAVE HIRED THE WRONG PERSON FOR THE JOB A FEW times. Making the wrong hire is a huge energy drain. You spend time fixing things, listening to people vent, and solving problems rather than growing your business. When you calculate the cost of a wrong hire, you know you must do something immediately. Some of your worst sleepless nights and biggest scars go back to hiring the wrong people. When we made hiring mistakes, we would fine-tune the recruiting process by asking, "What can we learn? What can we do better?"

When a solo founder tells me that they quadrupled their company size in a week, I think, *Whoa...was it really that easy to find the right people? I hope that works out OK.* When you are a small team, know that each new hire is a significant shift in your culture, for better or worse.

Recruiting is one of the most important things you do. When you start recruiting, you may not be very good at it. If you had the benefit of practicing your recruiting skills in a larger company first, that helps. You are always getting better at recruiting, and it's a key star in your Support Constellation.

There are safety precautions you can take, like hiring a consultant who interviews all the time. They see things you can't because they are so experienced in interviewing. Ultimately, you don't know what someone is like to work with until you have worked with them. That is why the ninety-day probationary period is super helpful. If you realize the person is not the right fit in the first ninety days, it's easier to transition them out. Just watch the clock. Don't decide on day ninety-one that you have a problem. I've been there.

Having well-defined, quantitative goals rather than qualitative ones helps make the ninety-day decision easier. For example, *bring in three new partners* is much better than *lead new partnerships*. The latter leaves too much gray area to know whether you have the right person.

When recruiting, look into the future to predict the reasons why you would need to let the employee go. Then, work backward to prevent that outcome. Method 29 addresses letting someone go. Two questions to ask in making that decision: (1) Are they meeting their goals? and (2) Are they doing it in a way that's acceptable to your culture? The first question is about if they can do the job and it's what most recruiting questions focus on. The second question concerns how they will do the job and if it fits your culture. This is equal, if not more important, than the first question. So, how do you hire for culture fit?

The first step is to understand your culture and priorities. Next, determine what questions you want to ask and what experience matches your needs. Often, small teams need people who can adjust, do many things, work well with others, work independently, and figure things out. Based on the candidates' responses, ask them questions like, "That sounds frustrating.

What did you think about working on that many projects?" If they didn't like working on ten different things while with their last employer, they wouldn't like working on your ten things. If you need someone who can figure things out with minimal direction and the candidate didn't get enough direction to be successful in their last job, keep looking.

Beyond questions, give people role-specific tests. How they respond to taking a test provides insight into their personality. We gave tests related to the job, such as scientist, analyst, and business development associate. For the lab, we needed people who were good with their hands, so we gave them an erector set and asked them to create something in thirty minutes. While it started as a process to evaluate how candidates work with their hands, we later learned that it gave us insight into their thought process, creativity, time management, and how they handled the request. If you get pushback about creating something with an erector set, the candidate won't like taking out the trash. By design, Orbis was a place where everyone took out the trash occasionally. We knew this about our culture, and we hired for it.

Here is a summary of a recruiting process I've developed over the years:

- **Identify what you need and establish a role description.** Putting it on paper helps you flesh out your requirements. If you don't have a starting point, search for the closest roles you have to use as an example to get you thinking.
- **Consider how much you can afford for this role and research comparable compensation ranges.** It's good to have resources to back up your ranges. You can find this by searching for similar positions and what competitors are offering. Industry associations provide compensation

surveys you can use as a reference. If stock options are a portion of the compensation, there is no nice, neat reference, but research helps determine what is fair.
- **Advertise the position where your candidates are most likely to look.** Know the differences between the different recruiting sites in their candidate pools. There are many places to post job openings, so experiment to see what works best for you. Indeed and LinkedIn worked for us. AngelList and Stack Overflow are often mentioned for tech hires. Don't forget to ask your friends, as one of our best hires came from asking around. Usually, the perfect person is just a second-degree connection away.
- **Collect and pool resumes.** Write down the screening criteria you will use when the resumes come in.
- **Filter the resumes.** Consider having a first, second, and third filter, depending on how many people you have on your team. If it is only you, ask friends to lend their recruiting experience.
- **Perform phone interviews with a set of questions you ask each candidate.** Don't reinvent the wheel every time. You want to compare answers across candidates. Our calls were thirty minutes long, and I looked for specific things we needed. I didn't want to waste people's time if they didn't have a core fit.
- **Identify your top three to five candidates for the first-round interview.** Send candidates an employment application and consumer report authorization form. Ask candidates for a written explanation of why they would be a good fit for your company and why your company would be a good fit for them.
- **Hold first-round interviews.** Ask your candidates to give a presentation on their professional story. Provide a test or

questionnaire to simulate what the candidate can do. Consider thirty- to forty-five-minute interviews with each team member when it's a small team. If it's just you, find a friend with experience interviewing or hire an expert to do a few interviews for you and give you their perspective.
- **Consider logistics.** If your candidate is from out of town, you may want to combine first-round and second-round interviews. The thought behind two different days is that people can be great one day and not the next. You get to know the candidate on different days with two different interviews. Two interviews may not be realistic when the candidate lives out of town. Make adjustments where necessary.
- **Decide if you want to go further with the process.** If not, go back to collecting resumes.
- **Perform due diligence on the candidate.** Do a basic internet search. It's embarrassing if you skip this step and find something you don't want to see later. Call their references. Outsource the background search (e.g., ACS Data Search for a criminal background check, social security verification, address trace, and degree verification).
- **Prepare for a second-round interview.** Ask the candidate to take a role-fit test (e.g., DiSC, Culture Fit, etc.), and hire an expert consultant to guide you on fit or if there are areas to probe.
- **Hold second-round interviews.** Provide any additional interviews appropriate for the role. Our HR consultant and other consultants interviewed candidates. Repeat more in-depth interviews with team members as appropriate. Discuss the applicant's impression of your company and the job opening to determine fit.
- **Gather feedback separately from all the interviewers.** If

they talk to each other before you speak to them, they can influence each other's perspective.
- **Decide on your top candidate and a backup candidate.** Review your initial criteria in making this decision.
- **Extend the offer with excitement!** Know that you still have the compensation package negotiation. Consider this as part of the recruiting process. You will get deeper insights about the person at this stage. They aren't your employees until they have started working. If you don't like what you see during the contract negotiation, consider that information to ensure they are a fit for you.
- **Politely decline the candidates that you don't move forward with.** The last experience you have with someone is what you remember the most. Extend the courtesy of a phone call thanking them for their time and interest. They may just want to get off the phone. Allow them to do that. If they ask for constructive feedback, offer genuine positive and constructive feedback where possible. I am always impressed when people don't get the job but still have positive things to say about the company and the experience. That is a worthy goal.

When you make your first hire, you will want to have these things in place:

- An employee handbook
- Clear lines of feedback
- A uniform, documented review process
- A performance improvement process

These items help to address when things aren't going well. You want everyone on the same page while providing an opportunity for the employee to correct their performance. Most importantly, you want clarity of what happens at the end of the improvement time under different scenarios.

Recruiting helps you give yourself a system to get the best people you can. Start with this process and evolve as you learn more about what works for you.

hiring BASICS

QUESTION	INSIGHTS
What kind of work do you like to do best?	Look for what you need (detail-oriented = project manager; relationship-oriented = sales lead).
What excited you about this role?	If they aren't excited about it now, they won't be excited in a year.
What previous work experience relates to this role?	Have them prove that they know how to be successful in this role.
How do you handle _____ (ambiguity, wearing many hats, etc.)?	Include the most challenging parts of the role and ask them to follow up.
What is your problem-solving process?	Give them a specific example problem to solve and see if it fits into what you need.
When was a time you had to handle a difficult situation at work? How did you handle it?	You want to know how they will work with you and the other people on your team.
How do you prioritize and manage your workload?	This is super important when they have a lot to get done.
What was a recent time that you failed? What did you learn from it?	You want to make sure they aren't afraid of failure and they won't repeat it.
How do you handle tight deadlines or high-pressure situations?	Gather insights into what it will be like to work with them.
When was a recent time you had to adapt to a new technology or tool?	You want to see how adaptive they are and what kind of self-learner they are.
What are your greatest strengths and weaknesses?	See how self-aware they are.
What compensation expectations do you have?	If they need 10 times what you have to offer, this question can save you both time.
What questions do you have?	It is always a warning sign if they don't have questions.

Template Notes

You can download a printable version of this template at: makeopportunityhappen.com/templates/18

These are sample **questions** to get you started on your interview list and the **insight** to look for. Use the questions that work for your business and add to them to create your own go-to recruiting questions.

RECAP

The top four ways to recruit to align your stars:

1. Realize that recruiting is one of the most important things you do.
2. Create a recruiting process and follow it.
3. Have a set list of recruiting questions (Template 18) that helps you treat candidates equitably, compare candidates, and identify trends for an efficient hiring process.
4. Improve your recruiting process by finding things that work for you and making changes when encountering mistakes.

RESOURCES

- Build a Team by Cooley GO: https://www.cooleygo.com/topic/build-a-team/
- Offer Letter and Employment Agreement Package by Cooley GO https://www.cooleygo.com/documents/new-employee-package-uk/
- *The Essential HR Handbook, 10th Anniversary Edition: A Quick and Handy Resource for Any Manager or HR Professional* by Sharon Armstrong and Barbara Mitchell

HIRING BASICS · 163

* * *

Part of recruiting is choosing the right board to help you propel your company. Many entrepreneurs wait too long to establish a board. Let's discuss why a board is important in your Support Constellation and how you can start moving that star.

METHOD 19

Your Board

> *"If you are the smartest person in the room, you are in the wrong room."*
>
> —DECLAN FLYNN

I REMEMBER THE MOMENTS WHEN I ASKED PEOPLE TO JOIN Orbis's board. If you know them well, you can get a reply like, "It would be an honor!" If you don't know them well or they get many similar requests, you can see a look of panic in their eyes, revealing *What am I getting myself into?* I know this because I have both received this reaction and given these responses to other people. Board roles aren't something to take lightly. It's a much easier decision to make when you know someone and what they are like to work with.

Entrepreneurs are often worried about the idea of a board. Common thinking is, *You want me to get a group of people who can tell me what to do, when to do it, and even fire me? Who wants one of those? No, thank you!* Then, entrepreneurs keep muscling it out themselves, having to know better than everyone else about everything. Entrepreneurs miss the boat with this mindset.

A better way is to identify, set up, and manage a board that propels your company. Boards help you hone strategy, make connections, and provide industry insights. When you raise money, you will need to take the board seriously. If you know it's coming, why not implement one that can help you now? Your board is a key star in your Support Constellation.

There is a difference between a fiduciary board (think governance) and an advisory board (think guidance). The main thing to know is the responsibility difference and, therefore, the control a fiduciary board has over voting rights.

A fiduciary board is responsible for the financial and legal obligations of the company. This board provides independent and objective oversight of a company's management, strategy, and operations. They provide governance, which manages the company, including lines of authority, transparent communication, and reporting. Governance maximizes shareholder value, and when you are a large (or the largest) shareholder, that is good for you. A fiduciary board ensures an efficient, transparent, and well-run business.

An advisory board provides guidance to the organization. This board doesn't have the financial or legal responsibilities. Board members are experts in your field and have knowledge and networks that can be very helpful. These advisors provide input into your strategy and direction.

Some CEOs choose to have a fiduciary board and a separate advisory board. That can be a lot to manage. Orbis had a blend with a fiduciary board that also provided strategic guidance. Its function was both governance and guidance.

The best way to build a successful company is to have the support of smart people around you. People give you more support when they are on your board. Get the best people around you. Find people who have great ideas and robust networks. Get people who have seen the movie—like the one you are in—before and can help guide you to the movie ending you want.

If you don't take advantage of having a great board, you are missing one of your greatest assets. To maximize the benefit, decide what skills could help you, and that depends on your business. Skill sets to consider are someone who represents the client's mindset or investor's mindset if you know you will need investment. You want people who know the industry. Sometimes, having someone outside of the industry who can offer an outside perspective is helpful. You just have to make sure you don't spend most of your time educating this person, or their input becomes distracting.

Think about your most important functions. If you are a technology company, someone with technical chops is helpful. Someone with sales, partnering, and business development experience is essential. Advisors with a vision of where the industry is going are priceless.

Get people who have:

- Done the things that you want to do. People who have actually *done it* before and not just watched it or taught it.
- LOTS of RECENT experience. Get people who have context for current markets or technology and know where the industry is going and how to overcome hurdles.
- A variety of experience, perspective, and risk tolerance.
- A shared vision and alignment of where you want the company to go, the type of culture that is important, and shared belief in the mission and values.
- Credentials and reputations that when people hear they are on your board, they say, "Wow! You got HER?"
- A network that helps you. An ideal board will have a broad reach to connect you to the people important to your company.

You get better results when you have diversity on your board, and it helps in future recruiting as it expands your pool of interested candidates when they see people like themselves associated with the company.[8] On a small board, you won't check every box. Figure out the most important areas you want to have and start there.

Make yourself chairman of the board unless there is someone you trust with your life, and having them as chairman would propel your company. Pick the other four skill sets that you need. Brainstorm a list of people who fit these four buckets. You probably don't know them all yet, so ask as many friends as possible. It's reasonable to say, "I'm looking for someone who has done A, knows B, or has lived C." The more specific you are, the better the chance someone will say, "Oh, you should meet Z!"

Before you ask them to join your board, get to know them. Let them see what it's like to work with you, and you can see what it's like to work with them. Let them see you are not a psychopath or will call them daily for a pep talk. Give them stock options and treat them how they want to be treated. Respect their time and send them review materials well in advance so they have time to go through them. Don't put them through fire drills.

People want to join missions they believe in, people they respect, and companies with real potential. Besides you and your team, your best sales tool in attracting board members is the other people around the boardroom table. People like to be around other people who they respect and admire. That is

---

8   Sundiatu Dixon-Fyle, Kevin Dolan, Dame Vivian Hunt, and Sara Prince, *Diversity Wins: How Inclusion Matters* (McKinsey Report, May 2020), https://www.mckinsey.com/featured-insights/diversity-and-inclusion/diversity-wins-how-inclusion-matters.

why it's essential to consider what each director will bring and how the board will function as a group. Having a director where people say, "Wow! You got HIM?" helps to get other directors who are also "WOW!"

Building a board is like building a team, and culture is important. This is another reason to get to know the potential board members before you invite them onto the board. Be thoughtful about how the personalities will mix. Don't let one individual dominate the entire conversation where the rest of the board can't get a word in. You want the board members to have a baseline understanding of what you are doing so you don't spend 90 percent of the time educating them. Get people with different backgrounds and perspectives to make the best decisions. Make sure they fit your company's culture.

Now that you have a board, what do you do with it? Establish regular, quarterly meetings. Set a standard agenda and send prep materials beforehand. The meeting's purpose is to have your directors help you solve problems and seize opportunities. It's not for you to do a big song and dance. This is difficult because you feel that you need to tell them all the details. You want validation that you are doing the right things. Try hard to limit what you say and listen to what they say. Structure the questions and discussion to what is most helpful for you. Don't let the directors take the conversation all over the place. Guide them to questions that will help you the most right now. Send the board the questions beforehand to have them in mind before they come to the meeting.

An example agenda is:

- Update
    - Priorities: a dashboard summarizing the top five priorities and then the next top five priorities

- Financial dashboard and cash position
- Discussion
    - The important topics that you need to talk about regarding strategy, direction, and next steps
- Actions
    - What do you need to vote on (for a fiduciary board)?

Have one-on-one conversations with your board members on specific topics. Outline who you are going to for what topics beforehand so you have an automatic process. Otherwise, you'll forget that you have this great brain trust.

Show off your board. If you have selected them correctly, they have credentials to help you. Include them in your presentation, on your website, and whatever is most appropriate. Get their approval on what you post before you post it.

Ask your board members for help because they want you to succeed. They can help you only if they know about your opportunities and challenges. Ask your board members for introductions and make it easy for them (see Method 20).

Don't waste their time. Everyone has a certain amount of time they can give. Start with your highest priority items. If there is more time, work your way down the list.

Identify, set up, and run a board that propels your company.

YOUR *board*

19

COMMON VALUES

NAME

_____
_____
_____
_____
_____

DIVERSE SKILLS AND EXPERIENCE

NAME

FINANCE
INDUSTRY
TECHNOLOGY
LEGAL
STRATEGY
BUSINESS DEVELOPMENT
MARKETING
LEADERSHIP/GOVERNANCE
_____

Template Notes

You can download a printable version of this template at:
makeopportunityhappen.com/templates/19

In the top part, list your **common values**, ambitions, and plans for the future that you want everyone on your board to have, and mark the people who possess those qualities. In the bottom part, map out the board's **diversity in skills and experience**. Prioritize the most important boxes that you want to check and start there.

RECAP

The top four ways to leverage your board to align your stars:

1. Leverage your board to help hone strategy, make connections, and provide industry insights.
2. Build a variety of experience, perspective, and risk tolerance around the table.
3. Use Template 19 to distill important commonalities among your board and areas of diversity.
4. Establish regular quarterly meetings, have one-on-one conversations with your board members on specific topics, and ask them for help.

RESOURCES

- How to Run an Early-Stage Board Meeting
- *Startup Boards: Getting the Most Out of Your Board of Directors* by Brad Feld, Matt Blumberg, et al.

* * *

A board is one of the most helpful stars in your Support Constellation. Having many friends in different places also helps you align your stars. We call it *Friendshelp*: the ultimate rocket fuel of friendship crossed with help that supercharges star alignment.

METHOD 20

Friendshelp

> *"I get by with a little help from my friends."*
> —JOHN LENNON AND PAUL MCCARTNEY OF THE BEATLES

IN 2009, I JOINED A GROUP CALLED PIPELINE ENTREPREneurs. Pipeline is a fellowship for high-growth entrepreneurs across Kansas, Missouri, and Nebraska. In starting the year-long program, I didn't know that this group would still be so important fifteen years later. These people cheer you on, feel your pain, and celebrate your wins. Like all things, you get out of it what you put into it.

You can never have too many friends. Not everyone will be cheering for you, but it makes it much more fun when you have a group on the sidelines cheering you to go the extra mile. it's also fun to be on their sidelines, cheering them on. You magnify your experiences when you share them.

Friendshelp is friendship crossed with help that creates the ultimate rocket fuel. You help your friends, and your friends help you. You don't keep score or expect anything in return. It's nice when the help flows both ways. This star in your Support Constellation helps you align all the other stars faster.

Sometimes, you are so "heads down" trying to figure things

out yourself that you forget you know someone who can help you. The person with the answer can be so close to you that you overlook them. Put together a list of all the people with unique insight in reaching your particular finish line. Map the relationships that will be most helpful to you with their special insights and skill sets. Refer to your map when you are stuck.

Besides board members (Method 19), three specific kinds of entrepreneurs' friends are:

- **Peers.** We often look up to the people who have gone before us for their insight, which is hugely helpful. What can be even more beneficial are peers across the spectrum living the same things you are and figuring things out in real time. These are valuable relationships. When they have a company like yours, they understand your industry-specific nuances. But don't discount what you can learn from people in other industries. Taking an idea from an unrelated industry into your space is where some of the most exciting innovation happens. A weekly lunch or call can greatly help you connect with peers.
- **Consultants.** These are exceptional additions to your team and represent legal, accounting, human resources, marketing, and regulatory specialties. If you treat your consultants like they are a part of your team, guess who is high on their list to help when you need something fast? You are. There is great value in integrating your consultants into your team and culture. They are a part of your organization.
- **Mentors.** Your mentors are some of the most important relationships you establish. Here is a top ten list for getting a great mentor:
    - Ask around. A great mentor is probably a second-degree connection away. Be specific about the expertise you are looking for so it's easier for people to connect you with

the right person. For me, it was someone with pharmaceutical licensing experience, as I wanted someone who had the mindset of my customer.
- Pick one trusted mentor and invest in them. Developing a solid mentor-mentee relationship takes time, so pick THE PERSON you will benefit from the most.
- Make sure your mentor is a great sounding board. Often, the answer is within you, and you need a place to lay out things. Your mentor should listen more than they talk, and they should ask important questions.
- Put trust at the top of your list of criteria. Your mentor must add credible value to you and ask the right questions. It's a confidential relationship and a BS-free zone.
- Look for a mentor who gives you what you need when needed. Sometimes, it's encouragement. Sometimes, it's a confidante. Sometimes, it's a connection to someone who has been through similar things so you know you are not alone. Sometimes it's a good hard kick in the ass.
- Test the waters with your mentor before you go all in. They are a vital person in your world, so choose wisely.
- Pay your mentor when you can. It often starts as a free conversation so you can gauge the fit. Pay them in cash, stock options, or both if you want considerable time. Then, you won't feel like you are bothering them because they are also getting something out of the relationship.
- Keep a regular frequency with your mentor. Weekly calls with your mentor help you progress toward your goals (e.g., I'll finish these three things before I talk with her next). Also, when the holy shit moments happen, your mentor has the context of what is happening in your world, and you don't have to take time to bring them up to speed.
- Have a "board" of advisors. Even though one primary

mentor is best, having a set of five to ten advisors with different expertise, networks, and diverse points of view is immensely helpful. Take the best of everyone: be like one person in strategy and another in relationship building.
- Mentor someone else. Be grateful to those who have helped you by helping other entrepreneurs. It's energizing to share something that benefits someone else.

One thing that is worth thinking through is the "forwardable email." This is the email you send to someone with the express purpose of making it easy for them to send it on to the person you want them to introduce. This email includes a few sentences about why you want the introduction to the specific person and a few sentences about who you and your company are. This way, you get to control the narrative about your company and you don't have to correct something if it isn't quite right. Most importantly, you dramatically increase your chances of the connection happening.

Limit one email per introduction, and tailor it to each introduction. If you want three introductions, send three emails. Getting an email requesting introductions to ten different people gives your introducer a big job and decreases the chances of it getting done. Make it compelling for the ultimate reader, the person you want to connect with.

I saw an entrepreneur at a happy hour. In a two-minute conversation, I said, "Oh, I should connect you with my investor friends at SpringTide." Within two hours, he sent me his forwardable email for me to take action while the conversation was fresh. He could do that because his forwardable email was ready to go. It was easy for him to make it easy for me. I could forward the email with a two-sentence note right away. Steven Coen agreed that I could share this example with you:

Maria,

Thank you for being willing to see if the folks at SpringTide would be interested in connecting so we can get to know each other prior to going out for a round later this year.

I've met a couple of people at WellSheet who impressed me during their session at HIMSS last year, and I'd be thrilled to be a part of that high caliber of founders and teams.

Lastly, I appreciate their callout of the importance of Clay Christensen's work in healthcare (and beyond), and I think they would see some of the framework present in how we've built SaRA Health in comparison to our competition.

Attached is our teaser deck and a few bits of traction.

Since our first practice was reimbursed via SaRA Health in late July 22, we have contracted with 100+ clinicians across 6 practices with a contract out for a 1,000+ PT organization and a pipeline of over 1,000 PTs, OTs, and SLPs equates to $2.9M in ARR. Our average sales cycle for an outpatient PT practice right now is less than 90 days, and our latest investment was from a PT practice owner/customer. Our current patient engagement is high with 70-87% of patients responding to 16+ messages (billing threshold for RTM) in month 1 with dropoffs of ~25% in the months following.

All the best,

Steven

Steven's email is a great reference point for creating your forwardable email. The important thing is to have the email ready to go. You don't have to recreate the wheel whenever you want an introduction.

Friendshelp allows you to maximize your relationships to *Make Opportunity Happen* while also helping your friends.

⑳ FRIENDS *help*

FRIEND	EXPERTISE	TYPE OF UPDATE	FREQUENCY	HOW I REMEMBER THEM	LAST CONVERSATION

Template Notes

You can download a printable version of this template at: makeopportunityhappen.com/templates/20

Map your friends to your areas of need so that you have a reference guide for who to call when you could use a little help. Start by listing your **friends** and their areas of **expertise**.

You don't want to just show up when you need something. Think through how you will help them and keep them in the loop. Including them in monthly or quarterly **updates** can be useful. Choose how you will update and the **frequency** of how often so you have a plan.

This is a two-way street. **Remember** things that are important to them, like their birthday, their favorite things, how you can help them, and how you help people important to them. Make a note about your **last conversation** so you can pick up where you left off.

RECAP

The top four ways for Friendshelp to align your stars:

1. Magnify your experience and make the journey a lot more fun by having a group of friends walk with you.
2. Leverage the three kinds of friends that benefit an entrepreneur: your peers, consultants, and mentors.
3. Realize that sometimes the person with the answer is so close to you that you overlook them.
4. Put together a list of all the people with special insights in Template 20.

RESOURCES

- *How to Win Friends & Influence People* by Dale Carnegie, Andrew MacMillan, et al.
- *12 Rules for Life: An Antidote to Chaos* by Jordan B. Peterson
- *The Laws of Human Nature* by Robert Greene

✳ ✳ ✳

Friendshelp eases the roller coaster of entrepreneurship and is an important star in your Support Constellation. Now, let's look at the most important stars in your Adaptability Constellation.

PART 3

Adaptability Constellation

"It is not the strongest of the species that survives, nor the most intelligent. It is the one that is most adaptable to change."

—CHARLES DARWIN

YOUR ADAPTABILITY CONSTELLATION HELPS YOU REVISE AND modify your stars. No company starts with the perfect idea or product. It's through adapting that you morph the idea or product into something important.

The mindset methods are to control your Monkey Mind and free your feelings along your journey. You are a creative problem solver who hones your intuition through listening—your Listentuition. You will need to be able to quickly answer questions through Rapid Discovery, adjust your story to specific audiences, and negotiate to navigate your stars. You need to continually adapt your company to have the right structure at the right time and let employees go when you need to. Above all, you need to learn how to Fail Up to get the value from failing by learning and moving on from it.

METHOD 21

Monkey Mind

"Mindfulness is simply being aware of what is happening right now without wishing it were different; enjoying the pleasant without holding on when it changes (which it will); being with the unpleasant without fearing it will always be this way (which it won't)."

—JAMES BARAZ

SOME MOMENTS STICK WITH YOU NO MATTER HOW MUCH time passes. You can close your eyes and feel the moment. In graduate school, my friends Angie and Leann visited for an action-packed weekend. While on the San Francisco trolley car, I leaned over and said, "OK, after this, we could do the Ghirardelli tour, check out Alcatraz, or walk around Fisherman's Wharf. What do you think?" Angie said, "Or we could enjoy the trolley car right now." That was the first time I realized I had a problem. My mind was always planning, worrying, and taking care of things. In the process, I was missing the enjoyment of what was happening right now.

This is something I was aware of and worked on over the years. As a mom, my kids' bath times were sacred, and I would remind myself, *I'm never getting this time back. Savor these moments,* I told myself. But if I went back in time, I would see that my *Monkey Mind* would wander to strategies to get the next client or the upcoming, tough conversation.

It took me six years of trying to meditate before it became a habit that tamed my Monkey Mind. The Monkey Mind is a restless, cluttered mind that jumps from thought to thought, worry to worry, and distraction to distraction. It's scattered and circles back to the same thought, like a broken record.

Understand the power that being present gives you to align your stars in the Adaptability Constellation. Most of our mental anguish is thinking about something in the past or worrying about something in the future. You can be happier, more engaged, and more self-confident when you are in the moment. This includes capturing more information and doing a better job when you are paying attention.

Meditation helps me to be in the moment. Meditation is not the only way to tame your Monkey Mind, but it works for more than 200 million of my meditating buddies worldwide. Other methods include running, nature walks, yoga, journaling, practicing gratitude, body scanning, paying attention to your senses, mindful eating, or anything that makes you pay attention to what is happening now. Find what works for you and incorporate it into your calendar. Don't rush to see results. If you let your Monkey Mind run wild for many years, taming it will take a while.

If you have not tamed your Monkey Mind and want to do it, don't get frustrated when your mind wanders. Rather than thinking about it as a focus failure, remember that recovering your focus helps train your mind. In my early stages of meditating, I got frustrated every time my mind wandered. But that's like doing a bicep curl and getting ticked off at every rep. Bringing your mind back to focus is the same as building muscle with each rep.

It took me over ninety days of consistent daily meditation to understand what meditation could do. Then, one day after a negative event, my reaction was much different than in my pre-meditation mode. I realized that this meditation stuff does something! The challenge is that it takes a long time to notice something, and we wouldn't keep going to the gym for ninety days without seeing any changes.

Being in the present moment means you are taking in everything happening now. You aren't thinking about something in the past or future. It's all about now. You see in greater detail. You hear things you would typically miss. Being in the present is important because you don't miss out, and you can't torture yourself with regrets or anxieties. You are too absorbed by what is happening NOW.

While there is broad acceptance that being in the present moment is helpful for everyone, it's particularly important for entrepreneurs. Entrepreneurs carry a heavy load with increased uncertainties, challenges, and people looking at them for direction to keep things going.

One study showed that 72 percent of entrepreneurs reported mental health concerns. Entrepreneurs have an increased probability of having depression (30 percent), ADHD (29 percent), substance use (12 percent), and bipolar diagnosis (11 percent).[9] Awareness of this fact is helpful for us to watch for problems within ourselves and with our friends so we can get help as early as possible.

An executive coach can help you train your Monkey Mind. I have someone I send people to, and they always come back

---

9 Benjamin Lee, "72% of Entrepreneurs Suffer from Mental Health Issues. Here's What to Do About It," Minutes.co, accessed November 7, 2023, https://minutes.co/72-of-entrepreneurs-suffer-from-mental-health-issues-heres-why-and-what-to-do-about-it.

saying the best things about her. Remember that it's a business expense. You don't blink an eye when you pay a CPA to help you with your tax return. Yet, somehow, you think the people who help you perform your best are either a luxury or a signal that you aren't as good as you should be.

Self-care is not manicures and massages. It's doing the work, not doing easy things for yourself but doing hard things that set you up for success, like meditation, diet, exercise, and journaling. Coaches will often emphasize the importance of self-care, like intentional deep relaxation. When you care for yourself and your dopamine levels, you can be more productive and get so much more done in a shorter time. You can do in eight hours what you used to do in twelve hours using techniques to keep you at peak performance. Don't fill that extra time with more work when you've accomplished that. Fill it with relationships and other things that fill your cup. You are a human being. Not a human doing.

Being in the moment reduces anxiety, helps you capture insights, and makes you more self-confident. Try different methods to help you get in the moment.

MANAGING *monkey mind*

(21)

MINDFULNESS METHOD **HOW I WILL INCORPORATE IT INTO MY LIFE**

- [ ] MEDITATING → _____
- [ ] YOGA → _____
- [ ] WALKING / RUNNING → _____
- [ ] NATURE WALKS → _____
- [ ] JOURNALING → _____
- [ ] PRACTICING GRATITUDE → _____
- [ ] BREATHING → _____
- [ ] BODY SCANNING → _____
- [ ] SENSE AWARENESS → _____
- [ ] _____ → _____
- [ ] _____ → _____
- [ ] _____ → _____

Template Notes

You can download a printable version of this template at: makeopportunityhappen.com/templates/21

On the list on the left, check your go-to **mindfulness methods** or activities you'd like to incorporate into your life. Then pick your top three, and make a plan for the steps you can take toward making them work for you.

On the right, ask yourself how you are going to make it easy to **incorporate it into your life**. For example, putting time blocks on your calendar, doing it with a friend, setting a timer to do it at a certain time of day, attaching it to something you already love to do, or attaching it to something you know you'll already be doing.

RECAP

The top four ways to be present to align your stars:

1. Understand the power that being in the present gives you. Most of our mental anguish is thinking about something in the past or worrying about something in the future.
2. Use meditation to help you to be in the moment. It's a journey, not a quick fix.
3. Leverage other methods to tune into the present moment besides meditation.
4. Use Template 21 as a checklist of ways to be mindful of finding your go-to methods and plan how to make them work for you.

RESOURCES

- Headspace, https://www.headspace.com/
- Healium, https://www.tryhealium.com/
- Inner Engineering, https://isha.sadhguru.org/us/en/inner-engineering
- The Huberman Lab Podcast Focus Toolkit: Tools to Improve Your Focus & Concentration, minute 1:01, https://www.hubermanlab.com/episode/focus-toolkit-tools-to-improve-your-focus-and-concentration
- *Real Happiness, 10th Anniversary Edition: A 28-Day Program to Realize the Power of Meditation* by Sharon Salzberg

✳ ✳ ✳

Staying in the present is crucial for you and your team. Another essential element of your Adaptability Constellation is to let your feelings help you rather than let them get trapped inside you. It's a challenging method to master, and we will discuss it next.

METHOD 22

Freeing Your Feelings

> *"The only way to deal with fear is to face it head-on. Embrace the fear, feel it, and let it go. Free your emotions and your mind."*
>
> —RICHARD BRANSON

I HAVE BEEN A GIRL IN A MAN'S WORLD IN ENGINEERING, digital health, and pharmaceutical manufacturing. My university classes were mostly men. My brother forwarded me an article a few months before I went to graduate school at The University of Chicago. The headline read: "Math and Muggers: Why Women Don't Attend the University of Chicago."

I've been the only woman at many tables and learned to be myself and one of the guys simultaneously. When I hear something questionable, I think, *Wow, do they realize that is offensive to women? Wait, do they realize that I'm a woman?* I don't justify or condone inappropriate behavior. I believe you have to pick your battles and save your energy for the most important things, and you have to build rapport before changing perspective.

One of the ways I have adjusted to fit in is to have control over my feelings. What took me a long time to understand is the power of emotions. You want to find ways to let it pass through you. Rather than controlling it, let it propel you forward. This is important in your Adaptability Constellation.

Like in the movie *A League of Their Own* where "There is no crying in baseball," there is no crying in business, science, and leadership. Put me in front of a movie or even a sappy commercial, and I am waterworks. My kids know they can count on mom to have tears if anything remotely sad or touching happens. When there is nowhere else for you to let this out, it needs to find a way out somehow. I closed off negative emotions in business because that was the "right thing to do." Now, I see emotion as a superpower and the empathy it provides.

Over the years, people have said that blocking emotions is a problem. My aha moment finally came when reading Commitment 3: Feeling All Feelings, the third chapter of *The 15 Commitments of Conscious Leadership*:

> We believe that great leaders learn to access all three centers of intelligence: the head, the heart, and the gut. In our experience, most leaders rely on their head and neglect the heart.[10]

The authors go on to talk about how you should release emotions:

> Human bodies naturally release. We take in a breath and let it go. We take in food and water and expel them. Unfortunately, we have been trained to keep emotions from doing the same.[11]

So, you carry emotions around. Because you need to release

---

10 Jim Dethmer, Diana Chapman, and Kaley Warner Klemp, *The 15 Commitments of Conscious Leadership: A New Paradigm for Sustainable Success* (Self Published, 2015), 82.

11 Dethmer, Chapman, and Klemp, *The 15 Commitments of Conscious Leadership*, 89.

emotions, they find other ways to get out if you don't let them out.

When you go through tough things, like firing people or having people leave you, you take it as "part of the entrepreneur's journey." If you don't feel it, it tends to catch up with you later. A client handled stressful events well, and I said, "Wow, you are handling this so well!" It didn't take long to catch up with my client later in a health diagnosis. You need to take stock of the damage, feel it, and let it pass through you.

I have carried things for a long time without letting them out and have seen other entrepreneurs do the same thing. You chalk it up as "just part of the journey." Now, see the value of letting emotions pass. Keeping them in doesn't do any good, and it CAN do a lot of harm.

When you have so much shit happening and don't fully process the emotions, you wake up looking over your shoulder for the next shit coming your way. That isn't the place you want to be. Processing the baggage is the answer to freeing yourself from that tendency to look over your shoulder.

So the question becomes how do you properly let it pass through you when there is no crying in business? While we all value authenticity and transparency, your team will freak out if you are screaming every time you are frustrated, crying every time you hurt, and hiding in the corner whenever you feel fear. However, Commitment 3 of *Conscious Leadership* tells us we know that we just can't pretend we aren't frustrated, hurt, or afraid, either.

People want to see that you are human. When they freak out, they feel comfort knowing you feel this way too. Your team will also feel relieved that while you freak out, you also have a plan. When they hurt because an employee just abruptly left the team, they want to see that you hurt too but that you know how the team will keep going. When you lose the huge deal you have been working on for years, they want to see you bummed too, but you know what things the team will focus on tomorrow.

For me, a private place to feel my emotions is appropriate. They say yelling and screaming help you know it isn't trapped in your body. I'm working on that. They say ninety seconds is all you need to get it out. I say ninety seconds is worth it to not carry it around with you.

Talking through your emotions and focusing on your *why* is useful. You need to find ways to process emotions and help them move through it so you don't get stuck with the negative ones.

If you need examples, here is some inspiration for ways to release:

- Go to someplace that relaxes you (coffee shop, bar, park), have a glass of the beverage of your choice, pull out a big sheet of paper, and download everything.
- Go on a long walk listening to music or a podcast that inspires you. Bring your dog if you have one.
- Call someone who helps you get perspective.
- Sweat it out.
- Get out in nature.

Let your emotions help you process things. Free your feelings so you don't keep carrying them around.

(22) FREEING YOUR *feelings*

| WHEN I FEEL LIKE THIS.... | ⇒ | I WILL DO THIS... |

Template Notes

You can download a printable version of this template at:
makeopportunityhappen.com/templates/22

Maximize your **feelings** by having a plan. List your common feelings on the left and what you plan to **do** when you feel like this on the right. For example, when I am anxious, I remind myself that I am prepared and ask myself, *What is the worst thing that can happen?* When I am frustrated, I take a deep breath and ask myself, *What can I be thankful for right now?*

RECAP

The top four ways to free your feelings to align your stars:

1. Know that there is power in feelings. Rather than something to control, let your feelings propel you forward.
2. Realize that if you don't release emotions, they find other ways to get out, often in damaging ways if you keep them trapped.
3. Show other people that you are human and have feelings and a plan to move past negative feelings.
4. Use Template 22 to intentionally map out what you want to do when you get a specific feeling.

RESOURCES

- *The 15 Commitments of Conscious Leadership: A New Paradigm for Sustainable Success* by Jim Dethmer, Diana Chapman, et al.
- *Atlas of the Heart: Mapping Meaningful Connection and the Language of Human Experience* by Brené Brown

- *Twelve and a Half: Leveraging the Emotional Ingredients Necessary for Business Success* by Gary Vaynerchuk

※ ※ ※

Using feelings to align your stars reminds me of the importance of capturing your creativity. Once I started to study where and when my creativity comes from, I turned it into a more helpful tool. Creativity helps you maneuver stars in your Adaptability Constellation.

METHOD 23

Creativity Catchers

"You can't use up creativity. The more you use, the more you have."
—MAYA ANGELOU

WHEN I BEGAN THIS BOOK, I FELT I NEEDED TO RELEASE something inside me. The stories and lessons I wanted to share with other entrepreneurs kept circling in my head, and I needed to write them down. I felt I had a unique voice, but who am I to think I am an author? In exploring this question with other writers, the thing that made my eyes go wide was the answer to this question: What happens when opportunity knocks and you don't seize it?

The answer is: It stops trying to get your attention and goes to someone else.

This realization scared the crap out of me. I didn't want to see this thing growing inside me pass me by. I needed to grab that voice that was knocking. You need to do it too.

When you think of creativity, you first think of artists and designers. Entrepreneurs generally don't reach the top of the list, but they should. Much creativity goes into being an entrepreneur in seizing opportunities and solving problems.

Cultivating creativity as a superpower is worth doing. You can learn how they do it from the creative greats.

Structuring creativity sounds counterintuitive, but creativity is generally seen as something you must "tap into." Make a roadmap to get to those creative thoughts to align your stars in the Adaptability Constellation.

When capturing creativity, the biggest thing is to write it down before it disappears. One night, I had a great title for this book when I was about to fall asleep, and I thought, *Should I get up and write it down? No, it's SO good! I'll definitely remember it tomorrow.* Do you think I could remember it the next day? No! Who knows what fantastic title should have been on this book's cover.

Where do your best ideas come from? In Sarah Blakely's Masterclass, she said she gets her creative ideas, like the name for her iconic Spanx, when she drives her car. This idea got me thinking: *What am I doing when I get good ideas? Do I allow enough time for this activity in my week?* It took me a while to figure out what I was doing when I got my best ideas. This is how you can figure it out: go through your day, and whenever you tell yourself, *Now, that is a good idea!* Ask yourself, *What am I doing right now?* You can tell where your creative zones are when you have enough good ideas. It's OK if you don't have one central place. My most creative moments came at the end of a walk, after driving for a while, and in the shower.

Where do you get your best ideas? Is it in the car, shower, or folding laundry? For Einstein, it was when he was shaving. Creativity strikes a relaxed mind when you are thinking about something else. Look for when you want to pull out your phone and take a note. You must capture creativity immediately, or it will go away or leave you frantically recycling the idea in your mind one hundred times before you can get to paper and pen.

When you have a wonderful idea, you often find a single flaw in the diamond and throw away the entire idea. No idea is great from the beginning. The process of iteration and learning refines the idea into a great one. Getting started is more important than coming up with a perfect idea.

Once you know your creative zones, make time for the things that put your mind in the place where you can come up with your best ideas. Note where and when you get ideas, and ensure you have enough time on your calendar for these activities. Note when an idea is persistent, repetitive, and longstanding because that tells you how important it is to you.

Develop a method to capture your creativity. Have one place to keep your ideas: a notebook, notes on your phone, or a dictation app. If you have multiple locations, you will spend time searching and lose your creative thoughts. Also, have a weekly time to download your notes to where the thoughts belong. Otherwise, the notes get so old you can't remember what they mean. If they involve someone else, you will miss opportunities to follow up.

Capture creativity, but don't let it distract you. There may be a next great idea coming through. Leave space for this possibility.

Here are some activities that can help promote creativity:

- **Get outside.** Nature and fresh air relax you and are great sources of inspiration.
- **Take a break from work and screens.** Time away helps us focus on the now when new ideas emerge more easily.
- **Read beyond your industry.** Ideas from other industries help us connect dots in new ways.
- **Talk with people beyond your field.** Mix different industries and collaborate with people from other disciplines.

- **Keep a journal.** Write your thoughts and revisit them to find new insights.
- **Play.** Give yourself time for fun that taps into your curiosity.
- **Practice guided yoga.** Yoga reduces stress and increases mindfulness, both of which help free space for creativity.
- **Listen to a podcast.** Get your brain thinking about different things and get inspired. Try the *How I Built This* podcast.
- **Find new experiences.** Travel to new places, try new foods, and talk to new people.
- **Daydream.** Let your mind wander to give it the space to develop new thoughts and ideas.

Pick a couple from the list to experiment with. When you find the ones that work for you, ensure they are on your calendar every week. If you know that nature and travel get your creativity going but you never make time for either, that doesn't help you.

The other thing to consider is just letting creativity flow. You have the creator and the critic inside you, and one usually has a dominant role. They each have an important part to play. Don't let the critic overshadow the creator. Let the creation get out and then later inspect it with the critic's eye to refine it.

Capture your creativity by having a method to get into the creative zone and be sure that you capture your ideas.

creativity CATCHERS

(23)

MY CREATIVITY COMES WHEN I AM...
_____
_____
_____
_____

I MAKE TIME ON MY CALENDAR FOR IT BY...
_____
_____
_____
_____

I CAPTURE IT BY...
_____
_____
_____
_____

I PROCESS IT BY....
_____
_____
_____
_____

I ENCOURAGE IT BY...
_____
_____
_____
_____

Template Notes

You can download a printable version of this template at: makeopportunityhappen.com/templates/23

Think through where your creativity **comes from**. Is it when you're driving, running, showering, at the park, etc.? How does this time show up on your **calendar**? Can you make more time for this activity? How do you **capture** these thoughts? Are you writing them down or dictating them into an app? What is your daily or weekly **process** for going through your notes and putting them where they'll help you the most? How can you **encourage** this process? What great things can you do for yourself right after?

RECAP

The top four ways to capture creativity to align your stars:

1. Harness creativity to seize opportunities and solve problems.
2. Write down your creative thoughts before they disappear.
3. Use Template 23 to evaluate where your creativity comes from and how you capture it. Once you know your creative zones, make room for the space and time.
4. Have a method to capture your creativity. Keep it limited to one specific place.

RESOURCES

- Sarah Blakely's Masterclass
- *How I Built This* podcast by Guy Raz
- "Your Elusive Creative Genius," a TED Talk by Elizabeth Gilbert

- "The Surprising Habits of Original Thinkers," a TED Talk by Adam Grant
- "Where Good Ideas Come From," a TED Talk by Steven Johnson

❋ ❋ ❋

Part of capturing creativity is ensuring you are open to all the important inputs coming your way. You want to listen for encouragement and learning to align your stars. This is *Listentuition* and it's a critical star in your Adaptability Constellation.

METHOD 24

Listentuition

"A bend in the road is not the end of the road...unless you fail to make the turn."

—HELEN KELLER

IT JUST TAKES THAT ONE WISE VOICE. ONE ENTREPRENEUR'S story that sticks with me begins with an advisor telling her to sell her product online. Rather than going online, she decided to go through an established brick-and-mortar store channel because it was a shiny partner with a big brand. This relationship required exclusivity, so she had to forgo online channels. Sales did not go as they had hoped, and when she realized she had chosen the wrong distribution path, the company was out of money and time. This story haunts me because knowing who to listen to and who to ignore is part of aligning your stars. The problem is that sometimes you ignore who you should listen to, and you listen to who you should ignore.

Listentuition is listening for encouragement and learning, and it's a necessary star in your Adaptability Constellation. Listentuition comes from: (1) what people tell you and (2) the data you get from the green lights and the speedbumps. What REALLY made that green light turn green? What REALLY made that red light stay red? By being in tune with this information, you can create conditions for more doors to open. This is Listentuition.

There is a fine line between the good ideas in other people's advice and the stuff you just need to ignore. Hone your Listentuition for the green light indicators on your dashboard for encouragement and the bumps in the road for learning. This will help you understand how to benefit from the bumps.

To protect yourself from ignoring the sound advice and following the bad advice:

- **Find quick ways to test it for yourself.** Call experts, survey customers, run the experiment, and see what happens.
- **Scenario plan.** Consider what happens in different situations.
- **Check your biases.** Sometimes, the wise words don't come from the person you think they should come from. Sometimes, bad advice comes from people who look like they know the most. Don't let your biases lead you astray.
- **Listen.** Understand where the advice is coming from. What is their experience, and how credible is their insight? What is their baggage, and how does that impact what they tell you?
- **Beware of the lemmings.** When many heads nod in agreement, ensure it's true confirmation. Don't get caught in the current going the wrong way. When there is a strong personality or someone with power and influence, it can be easier for people to just nod rather than battle it out.

When it comes to other people's advice, know that it's easy to stand on the outside and think you know what someone should do. For example, people may tell you to change your business model, lay off people, fire a customer, and get many new customers. They could be right, but the point is that it's much more challenging when you are the one who has to do it.

Consider the perspective of the other person. With enough scar tissue from painful experiences, they can come up with many reasons why something will never work. Parse the information to differentiate between valid data and the data polluted by their terrible experience. It's like getting marriage advice from someone who has recently gone through an ugly divorce. They may need time to calibrate the proper perspective before offering useful advice to others.

We all have baggage. You can talk with someone in your specific industry and see how much they despise this area now after their painful experience. These people have some of the best insights because they have lived it. Filter the gold from the crap. Heed their information and experiences but beware of the influence of the scar tissue.

Some people have already hit a familiar road bump and can help you avoid it; others see patterns and trends. Sometimes, you rely only on the frequency of the advice: "No, we aren't going to do that because only five out of one hundred people gave us that feedback." Sometimes, that is the right call, and sometimes, you miss valuable insight. It just takes that one voice with the wisdom to give you the answer you need.

Advice is only as good as the person's depth of experience and accuracy of information. There's a lot of bad advice, and sometimes it's dressed in expert-looking clothing. It's one thing to rely on the deep experience of your lawyer or accountant and expect to take their advice at face value. Taking advice from well-meaning business people who don't know your industry is different. Doing what everyone else thinks you should do is impossible because you will have people sending you in different directions.

Only you get to decide to change course. Do not let others move you off your course: not investors, naysayers, or even your internal negative voice. The key is to be open and relaxed enough to receive wisdom. Don't get defensive. You are always learning, always improving, and always evolving.

Besides voices, listen to the things happening around you. Notice the green lights and road bumps and what insights they can share. Your green-light days encourage you and give you the sense of heading in the right direction. The road bumps are the times for learning where you gain insight to make adjustments. The key is to know when to adjust versus just keep going.

Here are examples of green-light indicators on your dashboard:

- **Market research supports your assumptions.** How can you leverage this to make progress?
- **Waiting lists of customers who want to buy your product in advance.** How can you help other people also want to buy your product in advance?
- **Customers buy your product.** What were they experiencing when they agreed to buy?
- **People make an introduction for you.** This indicates they believe in you. How can you translate this into helping others believe in you, too?

The green lights encourage us to keep going. They also provide valuable information on how to replicate it in the future. What were the other factors that influenced that light turning green?

The following are examples of bumps in the road and how you can benefit from them:

- **Customers pass.** What insight will make the next one a yes?
- **Customers, employees, or partners leave.** What can you learn from the exit interviews?
- **Skeptics tell you why it won't work because something else didn't work before.** What insight can you draw from that thing that didn't work?
- **Competition is beating you.** What pages can you take from their playbook?
- **It takes so long to close the deal, raise the funding, complete the MVP, or get the client.** How can you expedite it next time?

The speed bumps help us learn. Dive into why some things fail and what to learn from them. That is where the gold is. There is value in the struggle. It's like learning to read. You want a path challenging enough that you keep growing but not too hard that you get frustrated and quit. If learning is too easy for kids, they won't learn how to overcome struggles. You forget this still applies to adults. You say, "It shouldn't be this hard!" when struggling helps you learn.

There is always something to learn from the bumps. One voice on my shoulder said, "Wait, was that *failure* right there?" To which the voice on my other shoulder said, "No, that is just *evolution*, baby!" Learn from it. Move on.

Hone your Listentuition by looking for the green-light indicators for encouragement and the bumps in the road for learning. You can benefit from both.

(24) listen TUITION
LISTENING FOR ENCOURAGEMENT AND LEARNING

← THE GREEN LIGHTS: HOW TO DO MORE OF THIS →

EVENT	HOW TO REPLICATE IT

← THE ROAD BUMPS: HOW TO DO LESS OF THIS →

EVENT	HOW TO AVOID IT

Template Notes

You can download a printable version of this template at:
makeopportunityhappen.com/templates/24

In the top part, write down your **green lights** and consider how you can get more of them. Write down the ways you've learned how to **replicate** them. For the **road bumps**, ask yourself, *How do we not hit this bump again?* Then, write down the ways you can **avoid** them in the future.

After you've completed your list of green lights and road bumps, look for patterns. Are green lights more common when you're working with a particular person? Do you hit road bumps at a specific time of the day? What can you add to your to-do lists, delegate, remind yourself of, or make room for to address this?

RECAP

The top four ways to listen for encouragement and learn to align your stars:

1. Understand that Listentuition comes from: (a) what people tell you and (b) the green lights and the speed bumps.
2. Know that there is a fine line between the good ideas in other people's advice and the stuff you just need to ignore.
3. Use Template 24 to document your green-light indicators on your dashboard for encouragement and the bumps in the road for learning.
4. Develop an understanding of when to adjust versus just keep going.

RESOURCES

- *The Adaptation Advantage: Let Go, Learn Fast, and Thrive in the Future of Work* by Heather E. McGowan and Chris Shipley
- *The Outward Mindset: Seeing Beyond Ourselves* by The Arbinger Institute
- *Leadership and Self-Deception: Getting Out of the Box* by The Arbinger Institute
- The *HBR IdeaCast* podcast by the *Harvard Business Review*

※ ※ ※

One of the best ways to listen for encouragement and learning is to run experiments. *Rapid Discovery* is the experimentation method for finding answers quickly. It's a key star in your Adaptability Constellation. Let's journey to Rapid Discovery next.

METHOD 25

Rapid Discovery

"The more experiments you make the better."
—THOMAS EDISON

IN TECHSTARS, WE USED THE BOOK *LEVERS, THE FRAMEWORK for Building Repeatability into Your Business,* where Chapter 3's assumptions and prioritization exercise guides you to list all assumptions about your business. Then, you look for data to support your assumptions and prioritize which assumptions aren't backed by data. It's called peeling the onion. You take things apart, examine them, and figure out how to put them back together. The tough part is having a destroyed onion in front of you and asking yourself, *Now what?* Where do you go to find the answers?

Next, you look for answers to the assumptions lacking data, which is where people spin their wheels. You need *Rapid Discovery*: experimenting to find answers quickly. Be sure to have enough sample size in your experiments to get accurate information. Beware of making decisions based on too few data points, as this can lead you astray. But you need information to act quickly as you don't have the luxury of standing still for too long. Knowing your options for finding answers helps you align your stars.

Experiments are so important because they help you get to product-market fit, which is the biggest risk of startup failure. Only through the process of iteration do you reach something good. It's a key star in your Adaptability Constellation.

To determine product-market fit, ask:

- Are customers buying what you are selling?
- Are they buying at the price required for a scalable business?
- Are they remaining your customers?
- Are they telling their friends?

You know you have reached product-market fit when you have built a product users want, see people using your product, and you are making money. But before you make money, what tests can you perform to ensure people will buy what you are making? Experiments help you find your way to product-market fit and provide insight into the following:

- What customers' pain points are most painful?
- What are alternative ways customers solve their problems?
- Which target market should you go after?
- How much should you price your offering?

Primary research is the creation of firsthand research through original data collection. It's the strongest research because it's specific to the technology, service, or product you bring to the world. It's also the most time-consuming to get.

Your research method depends on your target audience and the type of information you need. It's often found through:

- **Surveys.** Online, phone, in-person, paper, or any combination.

- **A/B testing.** Show two different versions of your idea to determine which is better.
- **One-on-one interviews.** Be sure to structure in-person or phone interviews so you can compare them. Interviews often use a one-to-ten scale and address customers' pain points, requirements, and needs.
- **Focus group sessions.** Discuss key questions with a subset of people to build on each other's thoughts. Be sure you don't plant seeds in their mind or have personalities that influence the rest of the group, or it will skew your data and point you in the wrong direction.
- **Prototype testing.** A prototype helps people visualize what you are building. You can get customer feedback and insights before spending time and money building the wrong thing. This helps you quickly iterate and develop an even better plan for what you are building. A prototype could be a sketch, vision board, model, or mockup. The goal is to get feedback and iterate to improve your vision.

You want to think, *What is the simplest test that gets me the data I need?* Don't over-engineer the test. Also, don't cut corners so that you don't get data that helps you. There is always a Goldilocks in the story.

In designing a test, consider the following ten steps.

1. **Define your objective.** Clarify what you want to achieve with the test. Examples include validating user interest, gathering feedback, and identifying potential problems. Outline specific hypotheses you want to test to focus your efforts.
2. **Identify key assumptions.** Brainstorm all your beliefs about your idea. Prioritize the most important beliefs that require

validation and test them to discover holes in your understanding.
3. **Determine success criteria.** Decide upfront what success means so you aren't fitting test results into success criteria later.
4. **Determine your test type.** Consider prototype testing, surveys, A/B testing, focus groups, usability testing, interviews, or any combination of these options.
5. **Create a test plan.** Determine the who, what, when, where, why, and how of your test. Segment your audience into different user groups to get different perspectives.
6. **Prepare for the test.** Develop the test materials (prototypes, surveys, user scenarios, or A/B variations). Recruit participants who match your target audience, considering demographics and psychographics. Get diverse perspectives from people with different backgrounds and viewpoints.
7. **Execute the test plan.** Follow your plan, provide clear instructions to participants, and watch the process.
8. **Collect data and analyze the results.** Gather the data and summarize what you've learned. Determine whether the data validates your assumptions and what changes are necessary. Use both quantitative data (numbers) and qualitative data (feedback).
9. **Draw conclusions and plan your next steps.** Based on your conclusions, decide how to proceed. This could include more testing, refinement, pivoting, or moving forward with data to support you.
10. **Iterate.** Repeat the process as necessary. Review your testing process for improvement.

Throughout the test plan, look for surprises. You don't want to filter data to only confirm your thinking. Look for data that disproves it. That is the true value of testing. Find the surprises early.

Secondary research is piggybacking off of other research someone else has already gathered. This includes:

- Published reports, scientific journals, presentations, and press
- Competitor information, including websites, marketing materials, and annual reports of public companies
- Online forums, Q&A, and comments

If you need a test plan for your secondary research, consider the ten-step plan for primary research and replace steps four to seven with an online research dive.

Think of it like a maze. When you get stuck, you keep coming back to the same question. Ask yourself, *What is the right experiment to get quick answers?* rather than *What is the answer?* You can easily spend thirty, sixty, ninety days or more contemplating the right answer when the right experiment can give you the answer in a week and tell you which way to go.

Important things to remember:

- Test one thing at a time to know which variable causes the change in your results.
- Get to action quickly, as data from an experiment can help inform the next steps.
- Allow yourself to iterate as new information becomes available.
- Talk with customers and find the answers yourself. If you outsource customer interactions, you miss seeing the answer to a question you haven't thought to ask yet.

Product-market fit is continually evolving. Just because you have product-market fit today doesn't mean you will have it tomorrow. There are examples of companies that successfully evolved along with their industry, like Garmin, which went from boating and airplane GPS to fitness tracking. Many other companies never made the turn and didn't evolve their product-market fit. Remember Commodore International, Columbia House, and Coleco. You don't remember them? Exactly.

Running experiments is more effective for getting answers than sitting around postulating all day. The market will tell you where to go if you listen to it. The most important reason to find answers quickly is to establish product-market fit.

RAPID *discovery*
EXPERIMENTING: FINDING ANSWERS QUICKLY

PRIMARY RESEARCH

CUSTOMER INTERVIEWS
One-on-one feedback structured for max use

FOCUS GROUPS
Discussions that build on each other's thoughts

A/B TESTING
A/B testing to find out what is important

SECONDARY RESEARCH

PUBLISHED REPORTS
Scientific journals, research organization press

COMPETITOR INFORMATION
Websites, marketing materials, annual reports

ONLINE DIALOGUE
Q&A (Quora), comments (Facebook, Reddit), B2B (Trust Radius, G2 Crowd)

→ ANSWER ←

PLAN

QUESTIONS TO ANSWER	METHODS TO USE

> ## Template Notes
>
> You can download a printable version of this template at: makeopportunityhappen.com/templates/25
>
> Review the **primary** and **secondary** research options when you need to run experiments to find answers to questions quickly. In the table, write down the top **questions** you need to answer and choose the **methods** you want to use to discover those answers, prioritizing them by which is the best use of your time.

RECAP

The top four ways to experiment to find answers to align your stars:

1. Have go-to ways to run experiments and find answers quickly. When you get to a "How am I going to figure this out?" moment, use Template 25 to pick the best research option for that question.
2. Use primary research through surveys, online experimentation, one-on-one interviews, and focus groups. This is more specific to your question but can also take longer.
3. Leverage secondary research by piggybacking off other research someone else has generated. Look to published material, presentations, competitor information, and online dialogue.
4. Run experiments or analyze secondary research to determine product-market fit. Know that your product-market fit is always evolving, so continue experimenting.

RESOURCES

- *Levers: The Framework for Building Repeatability into Your Business* by Amos Schwartzfarb and Trevor Boehm
- *The Lean Startup: How Today's Entrepreneurs Use Continuous Innovation to Create Radically Successful Businesses* by Eric Ries
- *Zero to One: Notes on Startups, or How to Build the Future* by Peter Thiel, Blake Masters, et al.
- Paths to Product-Market Fit: review.firstround.com/
- 12 Things About Product-Market Fit: https://a16z.com/2017/02/18/12-things-about-product-market-fit-2/
- PickFu, www.pickfu.com/
- *Crossing the Chasm, 3rd Edition: Marketing and Selling Disruptive Products to Mainstream Customers* by Geoffrey A. Moore
- *The Lean Product Playbook: How to Innovate with Minimum Viable Products and Rapid Customer Feedback* by Dan Olsen, et al.
- *The Mom Test: How to Talk to Customers & Learn If Your Business Is a Good Idea When Everyone Is Lying to You* by Rob Fitzpatrick
- Startup Roadmap: 9 Steps to Repeatable, Scalable and Profitable Growth: https://www.forentrepreneurs.com/startup-roadmap/

✷ ✷ ✷

Experimenting is useful for learning what works and what doesn't in communication. Communicating your story fits your Adaptability Constellation because you always improve it and adjust the right message to the right audience.

METHOD 26

Your Story

"Communication is a skill that you can learn. It's like riding a bicycle or typing. If you're willing to work at it, you can rapidly improve the quality of every part of your life."

—BRIAN TRACY

I HAD DIFFICULTY CRAFTING ORBIS'S STORY INTO SOMEthing that resonated with people. We could do so many great things with the technology that I would get lost in the details. After a coaching session to help me refine my message, I went to dinner with my parents, where I pronounced my message was now, "Orbis. We make drugs better." My mom said, "Oh no, that is too simple."

Telling your story is difficult because your story makes complete sense to you. You can't figure out why everyone else isn't getting it. Making your story compelling, memorable, understandable, and free from jargon is very difficult.

You've heard it before, "You win or lose people in the first thirty seconds." Then someone says, "Studies show it's seven seconds." And someone else says, "Our attention span is much lower now. It's three seconds." Regardless of how many seconds, you do not have much time for someone to decide if they want to learn more about your company or not.

Telling your company's story is one of the most important things you do in your Adaptability Constellation. It's how you get others to come along with you, whether they are employees, investors, customers, or anyone in your journey.

When introducing your company, think of everyone as an investor. Some people will be actual investors who may invest their money. Other people aren't investing their money, but they are investing their time and attention. Everyone considers, *Do I want to take time here and learn more, or do I just want to change the subject?*

When it comes to a business, the listener asks themselves:

- *What problem are you solving?*
- *For whom?*
- *What is your solution?*
- *How big is the market?*
- *What is your traction?*
- *How real is this?*
- *Will this team be successful?*
- *Why should I care?*

And, you need to answer this in succinct, clear terms.

Include information like market segments, number of potential users, market size, and number of users. Numbers add credibility. *This product is for the 205 million scientists who spend 35 percent of their time retyping their work* gives you more credibility than *This product is for the millions of scientists who spend a lot of their time retyping their work.*

You want to make it as easy to understand and repeat as possible. You don't want people to stop and ponder. You want them to keep nodding their head with understanding and say, "Cool! Tell me more!"

Go further in the "So what?" What are things people can do with your solution that they haven't done before? What big problem do you fix? Include anything that makes it real. Showing proof through testimonials, case studies, or success stories adds credibility. This demonstrates the value you provide. Avoid anything that makes it seem academic, an experiment, a project, or anything that doesn't seem real.

You have one story. Make it consistent and credible. That doesn't mean that it can't evolve, but you want to be intentional about the evolution. Don't tell one story here and another story there. While you have one story, you will have multiple versions of your pitch and many ways you present it, depending on the audience.

Different versions include:

- **Elevator pitch (thirty seconds).** Concise and compelling—include the problem, solution, and your value.
- **One- and three-minute pitches.** Build on your elevator pitch with more information depending on your time. Expand on target market, differentiation, and market validation. The important thing is that when someone says one minute, you say it in one minute. It's annoying to hear the ten-minute version when you said you only had one minute.
- **Customer pitch.** Have a presentation that covers the needs of your audience. Why should they care? What is in it for them?
- **Investor pitch (five to ten minutes).** Expand your three-minute pitch with your business model, vision, revenue projections, funding needs, and return on investment.

Choose your words depending on your audience. Generally, you want to be jargon-free. However, if you combine two technical minds, it will be weird not to use your common language. Know the language your audience speaks and speak that language.

Telling your company's story is one of your most important things. It's how you get others to come along with you.

YOUR *story*

1. WE ARE SOLVING THIS PROBLEM:

2. FOR THESE PEOPLE:

3. BY (YOUR SOLUTION):

4. IN A MARKET WHERE:

5. WE HAVE BEEN ABLE TO ACHIEVE:

6. WITH THESE RESULTS:

7. WE WILL BE SUCCESSFUL BECAUSE:

8. THIS IS IMPORTANT BECAUSE:

Template Notes

You can download a printable version of this template at: makeopportunityhappen.com/templates/26

Outline the **key components** of your business' story. Work on making it concise, compelling, and understandable to anyone. Include statistics, specific names of customers, and anything else that adds to your credibility. Remember that making something compelling often appeals to our emotions, and using specific, concrete examples and information (like numbers!) gives credibility.

RECAP

The top four ways to tell your story to align your stars:

1. Think of everyone as an investor and answer the questions they are asking themselves.
2. Use Template 26 to make your story easy to understand.
3. Go further in the "So what?" What are things people can do with your solution that they haven't done before? What big problem do you fix?
4. Avoid anything that makes what you are doing seem academic, an experiment, a project, or anything that doesn't seem real.

RESOURCES

- *Building a StoryBrand: Clarify Your Message So Customers Will Listen* by Donald Miller
- *Unleash the Power of Storytelling: Win Hearts, Change Minds, Get Results* by Rob Biesenbach

- *Jab, Jab, Jab, Right Hook: How to Tell Your Story in a Noisy Social World* by Gary Vaynerchuk, John Hopkinson, et al.
- *Go Big or Go Home: 5 Ways to Create a Customer Experience That Will Close the Deal* by Diana Kander and Tucker Trotter

※ ※ ※

Some of the most important communication you do is in negotiation. The negotiation star is in your Adaptability Constellation because you always adjust to get the best outcome for everyone. Negotiation is both an art and a science and it's the next method.

METHOD 27

Negotiation Starter Pack

"A good negotiator is someone who's empathetic, who understands the needs and concerns of all sides, and who finds a way to bring them together."

—BOB SCHIEFFER

THERE ARE LOTS OF RULES ABOUT NEGOTIATION, AND THE advice can conflict. For example, to the question, "Who makes the first offer?," you can hear: "Be the first to put out the number to anchor high (or low)." or "Don't show your cards. Let the other person make the first move." Like everything, the answer is, "It depends."

My team firmly believed that the other side should present the first offer in a crucial negotiation. It took the other side so long to present their offer, and we needed to know if we were in the same ballpark. My mother-in-law provided my lightbulb moment at my son's soccer game one Saturday morning. She said, "Maria, they need a number. Give them a number." We found an artful way to offer a number range that we didn't think would scare them off and left plenty of room for negotiation. This included several scenarios so we felt comfortable putting something on the table and our negotiation partner had a place to start.

A good negotiation is something that both parties feel good about and lets you MOVE FORWARD. Negotiation skills matter in about every part of your life. This is an important star in your Adaptability Constellation, and negotiation is used anywhere from client deals to employee salaries to getting your kids to brush their teeth. I've taken negotiation classes a few times. Chris Voss is my favorite go-to guide for negotiation tips.

Getting "no" is valuable. You learn insight on how to move from no to yes, and you know that you are pushing boundaries. If you are uncomfortable with hearing no, it's often a source of your anxiety when it shouldn't be. You are so afraid of getting a no that you don't go for enough of them.

You never know until you try. The unexpected yes you can get is remarkable when you use this mindset. To improve your ability to get to yes, go on a spree of collecting nos. This helps you realize that nos aren't fatal. Reset what you think is appropriate to ask for and practice different asking styles.

Do as much research as possible. Have data and rationale to support your position. Include evidence of what has happened in the past, customer testimonials, expert insights, background, and predictions.

Consider where the other person is coming from. What emotions do they have? What memories do they bring? When they have big emotions, they won't care about your data. Feel what they are feeling and use that as a starting point.

Look for ways to expand the negotiation pie. What are ALL the things that are important to us? What are ALL the things important to the person you are negotiating with? You often just think about the main economic terms, where other aspects can be valuable. For example, you fixate on the revenue when the press release and client feedback could be more valuable. Expanding the negotiation pie gets more chips to play than just money, giving you more options and more moves.

Key questions: How can you help them look good in front of their boss? Will this help them get that promotion? Will it help them meet their goals? You need to have insight into the basis of your counterpart's success and put the pieces together.

Always have someone to answer to. For me, this was always my board. Even if the board will agree with your recommendation, have someone you have to answer to. Use this to extract yourself from the conversation and decide what to do next. When you are the CEO negotiating with a vice president of another company, the VP always has the benefit of saying, "Oh, I don't know if my CEO is going to go for that. I'll take it to him and see what he says." Don't let your counterparty be the only one with an escape route. Make your own route. This helps you to control the pace and gives you time to process and decide what is best.

Don't let your principles or feelings get in the way of a positive outcome. Keep your eye on the goal. We all have different approaches, styles, and perceptions of what is right and wrong. Everyone is trying to get the best outcome for their business. When you think of it that way, it's not personal. It's just business.

Stop the negotiation when it doesn't look like you will reach an agreement and have exhausted all the creative options. Don't force it. No matter how hard you try, you still need the other party to walk with you. Preserve the relationship. Tomorrow is another day, and you don't know what it will bring. If you keep forcing an unsuccessful negotiation, you will likely lose both the negotiation and your relationship. The timing might be wrong. You can say, "Look, I know that is important to you, and this is important to us. I value our relationship, and I just don't know how we will get to an agreement now. How about we keep making progress and meet up again another time?" You have worked too hard on the relationship to let it blow up.

Get better and better at negotiating. It's a skill that needs practice.

NEGOTIATION *starter pack*

WHAT ARE THE PIECES IN MY "NEGOTIATION PIE"?
HOW BIG IS EACH SLICE?

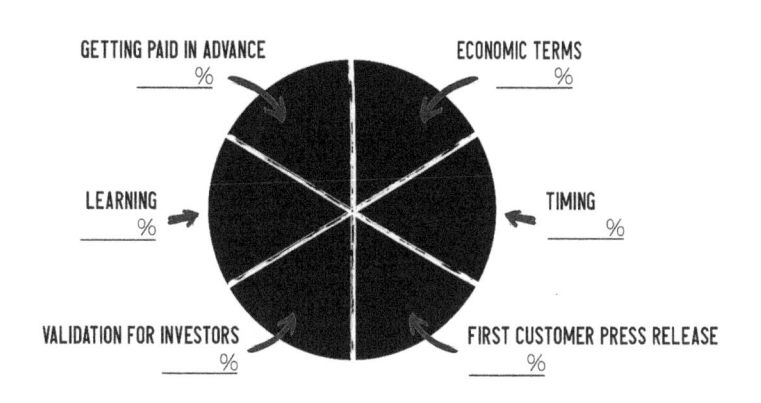

- GETTING PAID IN ADVANCE ____%
- ECONOMIC TERMS ____%
- LEARNING ____%
- TIMING ____%
- VALIDATION FOR INVESTORS ____%
- FIRST CUSTOMER PRESS RELEASE ____%

WHAT ARE THE PIECES IN MY PARTNER'S "NEGOTIATION PIE"?
HOW BIG IS EACH SLICE?

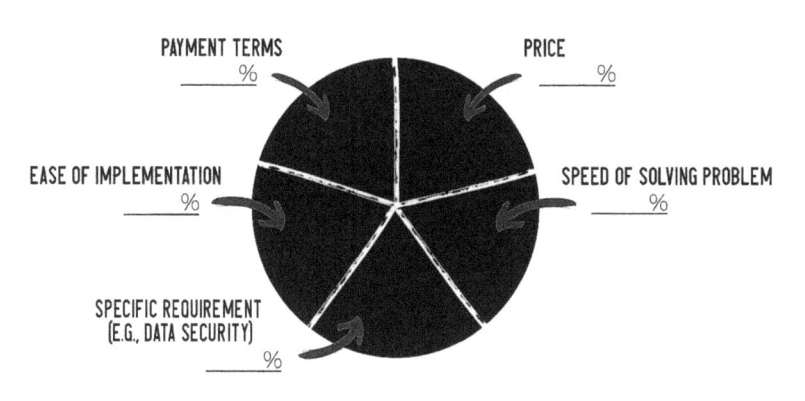

- PAYMENT TERMS ____%
- PRICE ____%
- EASE OF IMPLEMENTATION ____%
- SPEED OF SOLVING PROBLEM ____%
- SPECIFIC REQUIREMENT (E.G., DATA SECURITY) ____%

Template Notes

You can download a printable version of this template at: makeopportunityhappen.com/templates/27

List the **components** that are important to **you** and your negotiation **partner(s)** and their priority. Repeat this for each partner in the negotiation. Look for the areas where something is more important for one partner and less for another. How can you leverage the different pieces rather than everyone focusing on the same specific piece?

RECAP

The top four ways to use negotiation to align your stars:

1. Know that good negotiation is something both parties feel good about and lets you MOVE FORWARD.
2. Remember that you never know until you try, so get comfortable with getting nos.
3. Look for ways to expand the negotiation pie, have someone to answer to, and don't let your principles or feelings get in the way of a positive outcome. Use Template 27 to visualize all the components important to you and your negotiation partner.
4. Stop the negotiation when it doesn't seem like you will reach an agreement after exhausting all the creative options. Preserve the relationship when possible. Tomorrow is another day, and you don't know what it will bring.

RESOURCES

- *Never Split the Difference: Negotiating as if Your Life Depended on It* by Chris Voss

- "Never Split the Difference," a TED Talk by Chris Voss
- Chris Voss Masterclass
- *Getting to Yes: Negotiating Agreement Without Giving In* by Roger Fisher, William L. Ury, et al.
- *You Can Negotiate Anything: How to Get What You Want* by Herb Cohen

* * *

One important negotiation with yourself involves the right structure at the right time. This prevents both initial overkill and lack of structure down the road. It's critical for aligning your stars in your Adaptability Constellation, so let's explore this next.

METHOD 28

The Right Structure at the Right Time

"Continuous improvement is better than delayed perfection."

—MARK TWAIN

MY ENTREPRENEURIAL EDUCATION STARTED AROUND MY childhood dinner table. My parents would talk about the wins and losses, learning, and plans for what to do next. One specific example was when my parents found themselves landlords of an empty building. The tenant left in the middle of the night, at a time when other buildings around town sat empty too. They had to decide what to do while no rent was coming in. Twenty-five years before I would hear the words "pop-up store," my parents created one. They named the store Comfort Zone. When a permanent tenant emerged, they had a blowout sale. That is when I learned that a "Going out of business sale" made customers very eager to buy anything.

When I got around to my "official" classes in entrepreneurship, we learned about things like business plans. Then, when you get into the real world, you hear, "Don't worry about your business plan. It doesn't matter how beautiful it is if no one will buy your product." It's true. However, you do need to know everything you would put into your business plan, like your customer's problem, your solution, go-to-market strategies, and competitive analysis. But don't waste time on a document that no one will read. You can create a fancy document later if you want.

The *right structure at the right time* guides your Adaptability Constellation. Don't overkill the structure or fly with too little structure. Your company structure is *continually* evolving. This means that what was useful yesterday may not be useful tomorrow, but you build your tomorrow based on what you have in place today.

Examples of the right structure at the right time include:

- A startup doesn't need audited financials, but you need a system to show potential investors your financials and to file your taxes.
- A startup doesn't need a chief revenue officer, but you need a defined sales funnel of how customers go from leads to paying customers.
- A startup doesn't need fancy offices, but you need a place to meet and host clients.

Use the concept of the minimum viable product (MVP) in the context of the right structure at the right time. Call it your *minimum viable structure* (*MVS*). Take your website as an example. We made our first website ourselves over a weekend and our second over several weeks. You don't need the best website when you don't know if someone will buy your product. Get something out there, learn from it, and improve next time. Done is better than perfect. Make a list of what you would improve next time when you have more time, money, and people. Iteration is the name of the game.

In determining the right structure at the right time, Template 28 helps you decide what to figure out now versus saving for later. Take an item like employee onboarding, where you make your onboarding plan the day before your first employee starts. Often, you evolve your structure with just-in-time needs when it's the first time you do it. You build your best practices structure if you document it and evolve from there. Take the opportunity to learn from your experience. Even better, learn from other people's experiences. When you see a problem or opportunity they have that is relevant to you, put the structure into place to either mitigate the problem or seize the opportunity.

After you have picked an area like employee onboarding, go through a series of questions. Pick the three to five most important areas within employee onboarding to create a best practices document and add to it later.

Continually evolve with the right structure at the right time. Start somewhere and keep evolving as your company changes. Then, you won't waste time on structure you will never need and you'll stay ahead of the game in what you do need.

RIGHT STRUCTURE AT THE *right time*

WHAT BEST PRACTICES DO I NEED TODAY?
- What top opportunities do I have?
- What are the most pressing problems to solve?
- What do I worry about?

1._____

2._____

3._____

WHAT IS THE MOST USEFUL FRAMEWORK TO HELP ME GET THERE?
- Is it a best practice, system, outsource, or additional hire?
- How can I get to a first draft?
- When do I want to implement it?

1._____

2._____

3._____

WHAT ARE THE ITEMS I WANT TO INCLUDE IN THE FUTURE?
- How do I want to take this to the next level later?
- What time or other resources do I need to do this?
- What will trigger me to address these items?

1._____

2._____

3._____

Template Notes

You can download a printable version of this template at: makeopportunityhappen.com/templates/28

Use these **questions** to figure out what structure or framework you need **now**, and what you want to save for **later**. Consider items like employee onboarding training, customer acquisition, relationship management, strategy, marketing, sales funnel, financial management, intellectual property, or best practices for operations. Take into account your personal experience, or others' experience, and ask yourself how you can mitigate the problem or seize an opportunity.

RECAP

The top four ways to evolve the right structure at the right time to align your stars:

1. Use the *right structure at the right time* to start your business. Have just the right amount of structure and continually evolve it.
2. Leverage the *minimum viable structure* (*MVS*) concept. Get something out there, learn from it, and improve it. Done is better than perfect.
3. Make a list of what you would improve next time when you have more time, money, and people. Iteration is the name of the game.
4. Use Template 28 to decide what you need to figure out now and what you can save for later.

RESOURCES

- *Who Moved My Cheese? An A-Mazing Way to Deal with Change in Your Work and Your Life* by Spencer Johnson, Kenneth Blanchard, et al.
- *Masters of Scale* podcast by Reid Hoffman
- *The GaryVee Audio Experience* podcast by Gary Vaynerchuk

✳ ✳ ✳

The right structure at the right time includes the right people at the right time. When you don't have the right people, you have sleepless nights thinking about letting someone go. It's one of the most important things we do, so the next method's mission is to help you learn how to let someone go.

METHOD 29

Letting Someone Go

> "Firing someone is one of the toughest things you have to do as a manager. But if you're not willing to do it, you're not doing your job."
> —JEFFREY IMMELT

AN INTERVIEWER ASKED ME, "HAVE YOU EVER FIRED SOMEone?" I answered, "More than I care to count." Because I am a woman who smiles a lot, you may believe I'd never be able to fire people. In my first time letting someone go, a great human resource partner guided me through this process. Sometimes you get this kind of experience in other companies. Sometimes you let someone go for the first time in your company without the benefit of an HR partner walking with you.

Letting someone go can indicate a failure in your recruitment process so it's worth revisiting your process (Method 18). But you don't know what it's like to work with someone until you have worked with them for six months. Hiring the wrong person happens even with great recruitment processes. Also, employees can be very helpful at one stage of a company and not as helpful at another stage. Knowing how to let someone go is helpful in your Adaptability Constellation.

Letting someone go is stressful and how you do it reflects

on the type of leader you are and the kind of company you have. The first part of the stress comes from knowing when to fire someone. Ask yourself: (1) *Is the person meeting their goals?* and (2) *Are they doing it in a way that is acceptable to our culture?*

The first question is pretty cut and dry. This is why goals for each person are so important (Method 4). If you have clear, achievable, measurable goals, the employee and you should know where they stand. You should also have an explicit policy of what happens when employees don't meet their goals. Consistency is key. You can't have a person who doesn't meet their goals, and nothing happens, and another person who doesn't meet their goals and has to leave.

The second question, whether the employee acts according to your culture, can be more of a gray area. When the cornerstone of your culture is treating people how they want to be treated, have a clear, shared understanding of what is in and out of bounds. There will be things that you didn't know you needed to put in your employee handbook because you thought they were common sense. Everyone has their own experience and view of common sense. Continual feedback is necessary to ensure that everyone remains on the same page regarding company culture and policy.

Include statements in the employee handbook about acting with integrity and not lying to address future unknowns. You have to immediately act on certain behaviors (e.g., stealing) whereas other things are more about coachable moments (e.g., communication style). There are one-strike behaviors when it comes to workplace safety and handling of company finances. It's good to have a sentence to point to in the employee handbook that states the things that the company doesn't tolerate.

A good HR consultant is super helpful. This is someone you call when you want to double-check your perspective and consider next steps. In difficult situations, it's good to have a neutral third party in the room. An HR consultant is great for this. You and your HR consultant (or other third party) should take notes during or immediately after the meeting to document what happened. If the former employee gets a lawyer, the lawyer will instruct them to write down their version of events. You will want to have your version clearly stated in an employee file, just in case.

Because you followed Method 18 in hiring, you have these things in place: an employee handbook, clear lines of feedback, a documented review process, and a performance improvement process. You should also have an exit process to treat everyone in the same way when leaving the company. The process should be respectful of each employee and provide the opportunity to learn and grow as a leader and a company.

When an employee leaves, you want to make sure the rest of your team is stable. You want options of what happens next, including who fills what duties and how you will backfill the position. If there is a chain reaction of employee exits, your options dwindle.

Whenever a person leaves on their own before you need to fire them, that is a win. The employee saves pride and reputation, and other employees are not wondering if they are next. You avoid legal risks and financial expenses like severance, unemployment benefits, and legal liability. In a performance evaluation, always be clear on where the employee is and where they need to be to keep their position and provide space to either meet performance expectations or to leave. If the employee doesn't improve or exit on their own, follow your exit plan. Do not let an exit drag on too long. That's why there is that saying, "Hire slowly. Fire fast." A thirty-day window is often a reasonable time to allow someone to decide to leave a company based on poor performance. Allowing for an exit instead of forcing one can be a better approach.

Sometimes, an employee who was a good fit for the company in the past is no longer a good fit due to their interest, pace, experience, or other factors. Be grateful for what the employee contributed. Be clear on current performance expectations and exit planning if these expectations are not met.

When people leave, wish them well. Thank them for being on this part of the journey with you. Listen to what they say when they leave as it's an opportunity to improve yourself, your team, and your culture.

Letting someone go is stressful and how you do it reflects on the type of leader you are and the kind of company you have.

LETTING SOMEONE *go*

☐ 1. EXIT INTERVIEW

Have an exit interview form to gather feedback on how to improve your leadership and environment and give the associate an opportunity to be heard.

☐ 2. COLLECT:

A. Computer and passwords
B. Keys
C. Credit cards and any outstanding expense reports and receipts
D. Any files or other information you may need
E. Outstanding time sheets
F. Company-supplied materials
G. Address and email to reach them in the future

H. _____
I. _____
J. _____

☐ 3. PROVIDE:

A. Copies of signed agreements with a reminder of ongoing duties and obligations regarding things like inventions, moral rights, proprietary information, solicitation, competition, or anything else important to the company

B. Guidance and information regarding final compensation payment (e.g., accrued vacation) and benefits transition (e.g., healthcare, 401k, etc.)

☐ 4. CONTACT:

A. Payroll
B. Insurance provider
C. IT (internal or outsourced) to remove access to email and drives

Template Notes

You can download a printable version of this template at: makeopportunityhappen.com/templates/29

Use this template as a starting point for your **exit process**. Consider what other items you want to add to this list or any other process you will need to put into action. Keep your processes consistent, but always look for ways you can improve them.

RECAP

The top four ways to learn how to let an employee go to align your stars:

1. Ask yourself:
   A. *Are they meeting their goals?*
   B. *Are they doing it in a way acceptable to our culture?*
2. Have in place an employee handbook, clear lines of feedback, a performance improvement process, and an exit process.
3. Keep backup plans on how you will operate when an employee leaves and how you will recruit to backfill the position.
4. Use Template 29 and follow a consistent exit process. You have the opportunity to learn from the exit interview how you can improve your leadership and the working environment.

RESOURCES

- The Right Way to Fire Someone: https://hbr.org/2016/02/the-right-way-to-fire-someone

- How to Fire Someone Nicely (With Scripts): https://getjobber.com/academy/how-to-fire-someone-nicely/
- How to Legally Fire an Employee: https://www.uschamber.com/co/run/human-resources/legal-steps-to-firing-an-employee

※ ※ ※

Letting someone go is often a time to take stock and determine what you should learn. There are many times to review learning, and usually, you associate the word *failure* with it. Failure comes with a stigma, but it's an important star in your Adaptability Constellation that you want to learn the most you can each time. You call this *Failing Up*.

METHOD 30

Failing Up

> "It was okay to fail. When we were not failing, we were not on the cutting edge. If we were not making mistakes, then we were not trying enough experiments and that's a belief. It was okay to fail here."
>
> —MIKE HERMAN

THERE ARE TIMES WHEN SOMETHING DOESN'T WORK, AND I say to myself, *Let's do something else.* There are times when something doesn't work, and I transpose *something that didn't work* onto myself: *I am a failure.* The first outlook is productive and keeps you trying new things. The second perspective is crippling and doesn't help you to move forward.

People talk about how failure is such a valuable, insight-building experience. If failure is such a constructive thing, why does it suck so much? Isn't it one of those things that is good for *other* people but not really for you? The more you can lean into accepting failure and moving through it, the more you can learn from it and move forward. *Failing Up* means you get the benefit in spite of failure, and it's so important in your Adaptability Constellation.

After we sold Orbis and the transition into Adare was underway, it was time for me to move on. In figuring out what to do next, I wanted to work with entrepreneurs. Entrepreneurs are my people. Being in the trenches, finding opportunities, and solving problems is super rewarding. So when the Techstars Kansas City Managing Director role came up, I jumped at the opportunity. When they talk about drinking from the fire hydrant, that describes my time at Techstars. It was, "Hurry up, figure it out. Hurry up, figure it out." Then eight months into my role, Techstars closed the Kansas City location, and there wasn't a place for me. While the decision had very little to do with me and more to do with the reality of the business, it was difficult not to transpose this into the second way to look at failure: *This didn't work; therefore, I must be a failure.*

The local business news coverage didn't feel good either. "Techstars closes Kansas City accelerator as global network focuses on larger-growth markets" had my face right under the headline. The press for this story was much more than the press when we sold Orbis. I empathize with everyone going through lawsuits, bankruptcy, and other painful things that the media loves highlighting with a note that they "did not respond to a request for comment." Of course, they don't want to comment; they are busy keeping their world from falling apart.

They say, "Don't worry about what people are thinking about you because they are too busy thinking about how they look." But as I went into the community and talked with people who knew Techstars Kansas City, I saw in their eyes, *There is the person who lost Techstars for us.*

Plenty of things didn't work in my life. When I sat down to think about my failures, they weren't failures. They were just things that didn't work that taught me what to do next. Edison's quote is most fitting when he talks about his invention of the lightbulb: "I have not failed. I've just found 10,000 ways that won't work."

When you have an event like the Techstars closure, it's more difficult to say, "That was something that didn't work that taught me what to do next." I had a more difficult time learning from Techstars' departure. Later, I could see there is deep learning and transformation from going through these experiences. When you find yourself at the failure door, walk through it as this is where you really learn.

In writing this book, I told myself, *You can't have this book without a method on failure.* When I asked myself, *What is my biggest failure?* The ironic thing is that the biggest thing that came to mind was the thing I had the least ability to influence. I could have been the best employee Techstars ever had, and the outcome would have been the same.

The things that I had direct involvement in—like the pitch that went nowhere, the deal that didn't close, and the employee that I shouldn't have hired—didn't come up in my reflections on failure. They were just part of the learning process. Sure, I would have done those things differently now, but going through these experiences provided the learning to move forward to the next thing.

When there is learning and progression to the next thing, failure doesn't sting as badly. When there is not much to learn right away, and nowhere to launch immediately from that learning, it's harder. So the questions become, *What am I supposed to learn? Where do I launch from here?*

Getting the most out of failure and recovering from it starts by taking the time to reflect on what went wrong and why. This provides lessons from the experience. Make sure you:

- Allow for feeling (see Method 22)
- Rely on your support system (see Method 20)
- Pay attention to the right mindset (see Method 2)

Taking action often helps with recovery. Implement your learning and work on the fixes where it makes sense.

Failing Up gets you the value from failing by learning and moving on from it.

30
FAILING *up*

WHAT HAPPENED? WHAT ARE MY INSIGHTS ABOUT WHAT HAPPENED?
_____
_____
_____

WHAT CAN I LEARN FROM IT?
_____
_____
_____

WHAT ARE THE ACTIONS I AM GOING TO TAKE USING THIS INFORMATION?
_____
_____
_____

WHAT PARTS WENT RIGHT?
_____
_____
_____

WHAT MESSAGE DO I WANT TO SEND TO THE TEAM? TO MYSELF?
_____
_____
_____

Template Notes

You can download a printable version of this template at: makeopportunityhappen.com/templates/30

Use these questions as a guide to **learn** and grow from your failures. What kind of **insights** can you discover when something doesn't go as intended? How can you move forward?

RECAP

The top four ways to get the most out of failure to align your stars:

1. Realize that there is deep learning and transformation earned through failure. When you find yourself at the failure door, walk through it as this is where you really learn.
2. Learn and progress to the next thing so the failure doesn't sting as badly.
3. Use Template 30 to get the most out of failure and recover from it. Take the time to reflect on what went wrong and look for the lessons from the experience.
4. Allow for feeling, rely on your support system, pay attention to the right mindset, and take action.

RESOURCES

- *You Are Awesome: 9 Secrets to Getting Stronger & Living an Intentional Life* by Neil Pasricha
- *Failing Forward: Turning Mistakes into Stepping Stones for Success* by John C. Maxwell
- "Embrace the Shake," a TED Talk by Phil Hansen

- "The Unexpected Benefits of Celebrating Failure," a Ted Talk by Astro Teller

※ ※ ※

In assessing failure, it is helpful to realize that sometimes *shit happens*. As you journey from your Adaptability Constellation into your Perseverance Constellation, let's look at a framework that helps you take away the lessons without giving yourself excuses. It's always about learning and growth to align your stars.

PART 4

Perseverance Constellation

"Fall seven times and stand up eight."

—JAPANESE PROVERB

YOUR PERSEVERANCE CONSTELLATION IS YOUR STRENGTH to keep going and find ways to move the stars in the direction you need them to go. This is a long game. It's about finding smart, efficient ways to keep going before you run out of money, time, or steam.

    The mindset methods are to level set that shit happens and you need to find more ways to make opportunity knock. Along the way, there are important endeavors like selling and raising funding that are perseverance stars. Have methods to get unstuck and avoid the stress of not getting things done. Knowing what fills you up helps your star from burning out. You will want to keep your business from getting Long in the Tooth, prepare yourself for the Next Wind, and lean on others to get to your shooting star.

METHOD 31

Shit Happens

"Life is 10% what happens to you and 90% how you react to it."
—CHARLES R. SWINDOLL

AFTER A STRING OF CLIENTS STOPPED WORKING WITH US for various reasons, a board member expressed concerns and wanted to know what was happening. We dug into the details on all our client projects. We were completely honest with ourselves. Our post-mortem revealed that, indeed *shit does happen*.

Problems can happen for various reasons, many of which are outside of your control. You can work to prevent them, but sometimes you have to accept that shit will happen and the best you can do is to have a plan for moving forward. Adjusting your mindset to a supercharged growth mindset is needed to align your stars in the Perseverance Constellation.

A client can stop working with you for reasons completely unrelated to your product. You cannot control when your client has a bad year financially and needs to lay off employees, including your partner team. You cannot control when your client champion gets a job somewhere else and your opportunity to work with that company leaves with him. You cannot control your client's internal politics that bleed into your project and stop you from moving forward.

Other than your client leaving, other shit includes:

- Co-founder quitting
- Team walking out the door
- Funding evaporating
- Supply chain falling apart
- Company being impacted by floods, fires, and other natural disasters
- Investor derailing your company
- Poorly executed _____ (fill in the blank with a thousand things—animal study is the first thing that comes to my mind)

You can try to manage risks through contract terms, resource allocation, and diversifying your customer base. Sometimes the best you can do is look for the lessons to take with you for the future.

The bottom line is that there is a lot that you cannot control. You do your best and mitigate your risks. The rest is beyond your control.

Know that you aren't alone when shit happens. It happens to everyone. Have a plan to pick up the pieces, so you can move on as best you can.

As Friedrich Nietzsche taught us, "That which doesn't kill us makes us stronger." You get stronger when you keep going. A time that really hurt was when a key client stopped working with us because of a strategy change within their organization. If it would have been because we weren't doing our job, that would be one thing. But to stop moving forward when we were doing everything right made us say, "This isn't supposed to happen!"

When a devastating event makes you want to lie on the floor and never get up, take this basic formula to pick up the pieces:

- Feel your emotions so you can experience them, learn from them, and move on from them (Method 22).
- Have a core group of people who talk about it (Method 20).
- Revisit what is essential to you (see guiding principles in Method 10).
- Do something you love. Hang out with your dog, eat good chocolate, play your favorite music, or go for a walk, run, or workout class.
- Go to sleep and look for clarity in the morning, as things generally aren't as bad as you first think they are.
- Find the silver lining in what you do have and what you can do. Start from there.
- Gather your team together to discuss:
  - What happened
  - What you learned
  - The good things you still have
  - What you are going to do next
  - What you need from your team
- Get excited about what is next. Your team follows your lead. If you don't get enthusiastic, optimistic, and focused, neither will they, and you risk losing them.
- Try to keep up the good habits that you have. Bad events can feel like a chain reaction. When something terrible happens, stay active and double down on your good habits. Exercise, eat well, meditate, be around your family and friends, and take care of yourself.

You can't see the green light down the road when you are at a stoplight. You only see the red light. While you cannot see the lessons at the time, often, these are the times that teach us the most.

Shit happens, so have a plan to pick up the pieces so that you and your team can move through it easier.

(31) SHIT *happens*

WHEN SHIT HAPPENS, I WILL...

➡ CALL THESE PEOPLE:

➡ REMEMBER THESE GUIDING PRINCIPLES:

➡ LOOK FOR LEARNING OPPORTUNITIES BY ASKING THESE QUESTIONS:

➡ DO THESE THINGS I LOVE:

➡ MAINTAIN THESE GOOD HABITS:

➡ DO THIS SELF-CARE METHOD:

➡ TELL MYSELF:

Template Notes

You can download a printable version of this template at: makeopportunityhappen.com/templates/31

Use this guide to build a **plan** for when shit happens in the **future** so that you can refer to it when you need to.

RECAP

The top four ways to move on after shit happens to align your stars:

1. Realize that many problems can come up for various reasons. Some are outside of your control.
2. Know that you aren't alone when shit happens. It happens to everyone.
3. Use Template 31 to have a plan to pick up the pieces, so you can move on as best you can.
4. One star may have just burned out. Find another star to guide you.

RESOURCES

- *Grit: The Power of Passion and Perseverance* by Angela Duckworth and her TED Talk
- *Can't Hurt Me* by David Goggins
- "My Stroke of Insight," a TED Talk by Jill Bolte Taylor
- "Embrace the Near Win," a TED Talk by Sarah Lewis

✳ ✳ ✳

It's true: shit happens. But you know what also happens? Opportunity knocks. You just need to balance the shit happening with the opportunity knocking so the pile of shit isn't so high that you can't reach the door to answer it! Let's journey to the make-opportunity-knock star in your Perseverance Constellation.

METHOD 32

Make Opportunity Knock

"The doors will be opened to those who are bold enough to knock."
—TONY GASKINS

ORBIS'S FIRST SIGNIFICANT REVENUE AGREEMENT CAME BY way of running a company sales process. We knew it was a bit of a gamble because who wants to make a major agreement with a company that may have new owners in a few months? We were trying to create a situation where the client would flip to be a buyer, and we thought it made a lot of financial and strategic sense for them. The problem was that they thought about acquisitions in the billions rather than the millions.

But it was a very successful strategy to get the license done because they really wanted to finalize the terms with people they had known for years rather than a new, unknown buyer. So after months of back and forth and delays, we finally signed the license agreement. My coworker and friend hugged me in the hall and said, "I have just seen what it is like to will something into being!"

Those words have stuck with me. This experience was a test of perseverance, adapting, hard work, flexibility, and doing whatever we could to cross the finish line. When people say,

"There is no Plan B!" I don't know what world they are living in. Reality is that there often needs to be a Plan B, C, or D. She who has the most options has the most flexibility to get to the win. The *Make Opportunity Knock* mindset helps you align your stars in the Perseverance Constellation.

The key things we did to have a great outcome were to create urgency, help them out, make our partners heroes, be flexible, always make forward progress, and keep going.

Put yourself in the right mindset by knowing that you will get to where you need to be. Then, follow these steps:

- **Create urgency.** Our partner didn't want to negotiate with someone besides us. The fear of loss is a primary driver. It was a situation where they could lose if they didn't take action. This fear creates urgency.
- **Help them out.** Model numbers for them, give them the talking points to use internally, and help them however you can.
- **Make your partners heroes.** Think about how you can make them look good to the people they care about, usually their boss.
- **Know what you consider sacred and be flexible on the rest.** Know the changes in the agreement that you can live with and what is nonnegotiable. People are much more willing to work with you on the 10 percent you need changed when you have accommodated the other 90 percent of changes.
- **Always make forward progress.** Sometimes there is a term in an agreement you have already agreed upon, yet they will raise it again. Take good notes and don't let progress go backward.
- **Keep going.** You will get to where you want to be, particularly when you have a Plan B, C, or D if Plan A doesn't work out.

Making opportunity knock is the main reason that you do what you do. It's how you fulfill your goals with starting the company. Increasing your potential for opportunity-knocking starts with your mindset. You must know that the opportunity is coming. Be ready for it.

Increasing your chance for opportunity to knock includes:

- Showing up
- Following up
- Connecting with your network
- Helping people and asking people to help you
- Keeping your eyes open
- Listening for the signals
- Being informed of industry events and trends
- Remaining open-minded, prepared, positive, proactive, and persistent

Making opportunity knock is about finding ways to increase your potential for opportunity knocking and being persistent.

OPPORTUNITY *knocks*

TO INCREASE MY CHANCE FOR OPPORTUNITY TO KNOCK, I WILL...

➡ **SHOW UP IN THESE WAYS:**

➡ **FOLLOW UP IN THESE WAYS:**

➡ **LOOK FOR LEARNING OPPORTUNITIES BY ASKING THESE QUESTIONS:**

➡ **ASK PEOPLE TO HELP ME BY:**

➡ **KEEP MY EYES OPEN FOR:**

➡ **WATCH FOR THESE SIGNALS:**

Template Notes

You can download a printable version of this template at: makeopportunityhappen.com/templates/32

Ask yourself where you'll most likely meet the people or get information that will help you realize your opportunities and make them happen. How do you want to **follow up** with these people to stay top-of-mind when an opportunity arises? What **questions** can you answer to provide direction, and how can you ask people to help you along the way? What can you **look** out for that could be a potential opportunity (e.g., management changes, news headlines, opportunities others extend to you, etc.)?

RECAP

The top four ways to make opportunity knock to align your stars:

1. Put yourself in the right mindset by knowing that you will get to where you need to be.
2. Consider the key things to having a great outcome, include creating urgency, helping your partners do their job, knowing what you consider sacred and being flexible on the rest, and always making forward progress.
3. Be at the right place at the right time by trying things and showing up.
4. Leverage Template 32 to increase your chances for opportunity to knock.

RESOURCES

- *The Tim Ferriss Show* podcast by Tim Ferriss

- *HBR IdeaCast* podcast by the *Harvard Business Review*
- *Create and Orchestrate: The Path to Claiming Your Creative Power from an Unlikely Entrepreneur* by Marcus Whitney

※ ※ ※

One of the best ways to make opportunity knock is to get great at selling. Getting in the door is such an important star in your Perseverance Constellation that you will want to continually get better at it. Getting in the door is your next method.

METHOD 33

Getting into Doors

"Selling is not about closing a deal, it's about opening a relationship."
—PAT FLYNN (NO RELATION)

AT CERNER, ONE EXECUTIVE COMPLIMENTED ANOTHER executive saying, "That guy can get into any door." I thought, *What a cool superpower! I want to be able to get into any door!* I started to cultivate this ability to find the right person, the right approach, and the right win-win situation. Then, after you work hard to get in the door and they open it, you get a rush of "I did it!" feelings. It's like you are a kid again on your first bike ride without training wheels.

Selling is such an important part of what you do as an entrepreneur. You have to be able to get into doors so that you have the opportunity to showcase what your company offers. You get better at getting in the door the more you do it. Your preparation includes your approach, getting a response, and getting a follow-up routine that works for you. This is what you need to align your stars in your Perseverance Constellation.

When it comes to getting in doors, particularly corporate connections, you want to follow these ten steps:

1. **Have clarity on your specific sales cycle.** Adjust the typical stages of a sales cycle to be specific to your sales process. Typical stages include prospecting, qualification, needs assessment, presentation and proposal, handling objections, negotiation and closing, and post-sale follow-up. Often you jump to presentations and proposals and miss other critical steps of the process.
2. **Find the right contact.** Leverage the company's website and LinkedIn. It may be that there are a few roles that could be the right entry point. Gather your options and see where you can get introductions.
3. **Get an introduction.** To increase the probability of a great conversation, find a relationship in common with your lead. An introduction can help build initial credibility, particularly if your connector is well-respected. Make it easy for the person introducing you. Send them an email they can forward (Method 20).
4. **Get to your lead any way you can.** If you don't have an introduction, don't let it stop you. Just see how compelling you can be to increase your chances of getting a response. Offer something beneficial, appeal to their curiosity, and always provide value.
5. **Make sure your message matters.** If you received the email, what would it need to say for you to take the next step?
6. **Make sure your message reaches your person.** Use tools to see when the recipient opens a message. There may be an admin who is a gatekeeper, which is another reason to make your message as compelling as possible.
7. **Prepare for the meetings.** Do your research to understand their mission, products, pain points, and opportunities. Assemble a list of customer-specific questions for the call. Prepare yourself to do more listening than talking. When

you get nervous, you jump to talking. List your questions for THEM at the top of your page.
8. **Show them how easy it is to take the next step.** You often try to jump to the end where the customer pulls out their checkbook. Chunk your list of next steps. You only need to get to the next conversation, proposal, or specific *next* step.
9. **Have them see themselves in the driver's seat of what you are selling.** The easier they visualize themselves there, the more they want to keep talking.
10. **Follow up.** See Method 8. The key to follow-up is having a standard follow-up procedure, or you risk either forgetting about it or delaying it.

When waiting for someone to respond, never make assumptions. You can kill the deal in your head long before the other party has time to respond. Other people aren't necessarily uninterested. They are just busy! How do I know? Everyone is busy! They have a long list of things to do, and your item isn't at the top of their list. The question becomes, "How do you help them put that item higher on their list?"

We talk about escalation plans in Method 8. Have a set schedule that you follow with established timeframes and escalation strategies. While doing this, follow these steps:

- **Find out how they like to communicate.** Do they like email or loathe it? Will they respond better to calls and texts, or do they find that intrusive? Often email is best. An "If you don't reply by Friday, I'll call you to make sure the email didn't get stuck in spam" often accelerates an email response.
- **For those who think phone calls are too bold, remember that stuff happens in people's lives.** Emails get caught in spam or accidentally deleted, and people change jobs. You

may be waiting for an email reply when your contact has left their company. Calling someone else in the company can get you pointed in the right direction.
- **Always lead with a genuine "What can I do to help?" approach.** Finding ways to make this easy for them means making it easier for you to get to your desired outcome.
- **Have the goodbye email—the email that wraps up your outreach—as the last step in your communication plan.** Besides offering a "last call" signal, it touches on the fear of loss that the door is closing, and the opportunity is going away. If you draft it correctly, it is considerate and gives your contact either an out or a push to move your action item to the top of their list. The goodbye email works if you have some level of relationship, and it sounded like they would respond to you in your last communication. It generally isn't as effective in a cold outreach scenario.

The Goodbye Email example:

Hi Jennifer,

I hope you are doing well. I know you are really busy, and I don't want to bother you, so I'm going to close this opportunity. If something unexpected came up, and you are still interested—or if this becomes a priority another day—let me know, and we can pick up the conversation.

Thank you and have a great day,

Maria

Guidelines when you are drafting your goodbye email:

- Close the loop on the conversation so there isn't a hanging, "Whatever happened to…"
- Acknowledge that they have a lot going on.
- Don't make them feel bad.
- Replace "opportunity" with whatever you are working on—this proposal, offer, etc.
- Let them know they can reach out when it's a better time.
- Stop reaching out to them. It's annoying when people send the last call email, and they keep coming at you. Say what you mean. Mean what you say.

You get better at selling the more you do it. Key areas to focus on: getting in the door, getting a response, and getting a follow-up routine that works for you.

GETTING IN *doors*

Who are the people I need to talk with? _____

What are their titles? _____

What is their pain? _____

What do they care about? _____

How will I find them? _____

CAN I GET AN INTRODUCTION?

YES
CAN I GET MORE THAN ONE INTRODUCTION?

- **YES** → PRIORITIZE INTRODUCTIONS FOR BEST CHANCE OF SUCCESS
- **NO** → MAKE IT EASY FOR THE CONNECTOR TO INTRODUCE YOU

NO
CAN I FIND THE IN PERSON WITHIN A REASONABLE TIME FRAME?

- **YES** → REACH OUT WITH A COMPELLING REASON TO MEET
- **NO** → FIND THEIR EMAIL AND REACH OUT WITH A COMPELLING REASON TO TALK

Template Notes

You can download a printable version of this template at: makeopportunityhappen.com/templates/33

In the top section, get clarity on **who** you need to talk with, **what** they care about, and **how** you find them. Don't waste your time talking to the wrong people. Sometimes it takes experimentation to find which people are the best fit for you.

Refer to the flowchart when looking to open doors by getting introductions to people, whether they are partners, investors, or business customers.

RECAP

The top four ways to sell and get in the door to align your stars:

1. Realize that you have to be able to get into doors so that you have the opportunity to showcase what your company offers.
2. Use Template 33 to find the right contact and get an introduction. Then, prepare for the meeting, make next steps easy, and follow up.
3. Remember that the introduction is an important part of the process, so nurture your relationships.
4. Have a standard escalation plan that you use, including a respectful goodbye email.

RESOURCES

- *Sell More Faster: The Ultimate Sales Playbook for Start-Ups* by Amos Schwartzfarb, Sean Pratt, et al.

- *To Sell Is Human: The Surprising Truth about Moving Others* by Daniel H. Pink
- *The New Model of Selling: Selling to an Unsellable Generation* by Jerry Acuff and Jeremy Miner
- *How to Win Client Business When You Don't Know Where to Start* by Doug Fletcher
- *Coffee Lunch Coffee: A Practical Field Guide for Master Networking* by Alana Muller, Joann Bittel, et al.
- *Obviously Awesome: How to Nail Product Positioning so Customers Get It, Buy It, Love It* by April Dunford
- *The 1-Page Marketing Plan: Get New Customers, Make More Money, and Stand Out from the Crowd* by Allan Dib
- *The Psychology of Selling: Increase Your Sales Faster and Easier Than You Ever Thought Possible* by Brian Tracy
- *Secrets of a Master Closer: A Simpler, Easier, and Faster Way to Sell Anything to Anyone, Anytime, Anywhere* by Mike Kaplan

✣ ✣ ✣

Some of the most important doors you need to get into are the doors that help you fund your company. There are different strategies to get funding. Know all your options and use your time wisely. The funding star is in your Perseverance Constellation as it's a continual effort to make sure you always have the rocket fuel you need.

METHOD 34

Funding

> "Raising money is the art of convincing people to bet on you."
> —PAUL GRAHAM

EARLY IN OUR COMPANY, I ATTENDED A "HOW TO FUND YOUR business" workshop, and the speakers addressed angel funding and venture capital. We covered how funding works and the funding dos and don'ts. One woman, Donna, raised her hand and said, "What about Small Business Innovation Research Grants (SBIRs)?" The workshop presenter didn't know much about these grants and said, "Well, if you can go for those, do it. Nothing beats non-dilutive financing, but most people go the angel and venture capital route, which is why we focus on that."

I wanted to know what Donna knew, so I approached her after the session and said, "Can you tell me more about these Small Business Innovation Research Grants?" Donna gave me the low down on applying for grants. Her company had already received a few million dollars in grants and commercialized products. Donna was one of the people the National Institutes of Health called to speak at their conferences on how to do this right. And I had found her!

Funding is among the most challenging parts of starting a

business. But if there is one thing about entrepreneurs, they find a way. Sometimes you get creative on where the funding comes from. For us, federal grants helped us get the funding we needed. There are different funding options, and everyone's funding journey is different. Know your options to align this star in your Perseverance Constellation.

Often, it seems like we all read the same book and think we must follow the same funding path that *everyone else* follows, and we won't stray away from it. Not all of us are Mark Zuckerberg. When people are creative and take different paths, it often works better. It also takes courage. So many people get stuck on trying to get VC money only from the top investors, and they won't stop until they do. This narrow outlook leads to company failure. In reality, there are many paths to take. Let's first start with federal grant funding.

As the largest seed investor, over ten United States agencies invest over $4 billion through 7,000 grants to small businesses annually.[12] It's a competitive process, but it's worth a shot. Each department has a different acceptance rate, and on average, you have a one-in-four chance of getting a grant. Submit multiple proposals, and your chance goes up. Our company was able to secure over $9M over eight years. Looking back, we got 79 percent of the federal funding that we applied for, and it's not like we had a magic wand. We were diligent, stuck with it, and had great mentors when we started.

When you apply for an SBIR, you are working for funds nine months away, so plan ahead. When you get a grant, it's great funding. In contrast to what sometimes happens with VC fund-

---

[12] US Small Business Administration, "America's Seed Fund Road Tour Coming to the Midwest to Engage Small Business Working on Tech, High-Impact Ideas," Press Release 23-43, July 11, 2023, https://www.sba.gov/article/2023/07/11/americas-seed-fund-road-tour-coming-midwest-engage-small-businesses-working-high-tech-high-impact.

ing, grants are healthier funding because you use the funds as you need them, you can make good decisions, and no one calls you every day asking how their investment is doing. Plus, it's non-dilutive, meaning you do not give away ownership of the company in exchange for the funding. Besides revenue, grants are some of the best ways to fund your company.

With SBIR grants, people get scared with a three-hundred-page application guide and an estimated hundred-hour application preparation. They think, *I don't have time for this!* Do you think that raising venture funding is quicker and easier? There just isn't a three-hundred-page document to scare you from going the VC route. The data shows that 1 percent of companies get venture funding, and you better plan for much more than one hundred hours. The time and effort going the VC route aren't as visible as when you start the grant process. Just based on the probability numbers, you are twenty-five times more likely to get an SBIR grant than VC funding.[13]

After you check the grant eligibility guidelines to see if you are eligible and find an agency that fits you, call the relevant program manager to ask about the fit. Then start the process, and don't let it get overwhelming. Start early, chunk it, and keep going. Divide the sections among your team. We generally had three of us working on different sections to spread the load and to help each other keep going.

It's difficult to outsource the grant process. You can get help with guidance, grant writing, and reviewing, but own the process and think through what you want to achieve with the grant. You often think, *If we get a grant writer, that will speed it*

---

[13] Holly Eve, "Venture Capital Is Not the Funding Reality of Most Startups—Here's What Is," *Forbes*, July 6, 2020, https://www.forbes.com/sites/hollyeve/2020/07/06/venture-capital-is-not-the-funding-reality-of-most-startups-heres-what-is/?sh=fb3cc0a65ea2.

along. Realize that you'll spend time bringing them up to speed and finalizing what they do. Instead, block a few hours each day on your calendar, and get it done. People who do this well always say, "Even if we don't get the grant, this process helped us focus on what we really want to do and why." You flesh out a lot of questions and answers going through the process. If you approach the grant with that mindset, time is never wasted.

Not everyone's business is a fit for an SBIR grant, but this story is about making a plan and taking steps to do it. If grants aren't for you, consider early revenue, angel funding, and then VC funding. Early revenue is wonderful if you can do it. Let's talk about that next.

One pro move is to sell your product before you build it. Use this strategy when your customer has such pain that they are willing to pay upfront and wait for delivery. Often it's 25–50 percent upfront, a payment at a midpoint, and a payment at delivery. Whenever you can get clients to fund you, that is preferred. Early payments provide validation that customers want what you are offering. Think through chunking your progress. What is something smaller that the client can pay you for while you are marching toward bigger things? If you can't find a way to make early revenue or grant funding an early option, angel investors are usually the next place to look.

When thinking about outside investment, be clear on how much money you need, what milestones you will achieve with that money, and what happens next. When you think about angel funding vs. venture capital, a key question to ask is, "What happens when I get this money and achieve the next milestones?" If the answer is, "I need to raise more money to achieve the next set of milestones, and then raise more money to achieve the next set of milestones," your company could be a fit for venture capital. If the answer is, "I really just need one round of financing, and then we can grow organically from there," angel funding is a better fit, and you shouldn't waste your time with venture capital.

Angel capital is called angel for a reason. They come in to help lift you when you need it. You need to prove something with your technology before clients will buy, and angel funding helps solve this. Angels invest independently, as part of a syndicate, or as an angel group. Get to know your local angels and those most interested in your work. They often have experience and networks that are even more helpful than their capital.

Angels often don't post "Angel investor" in their LinkedIn profile. That doesn't mean LinkedIn isn't a great place to find them. Search for successful people who have an interest in your field. If you are beyond angel investors and it's time to think about venture funding, know what you are getting into.

Venture Capital (VC) investors want to invest in proven people with huge market opportunities. They want to make a lot of money and look smart. This is where your network of friends is handy as they can help speak for you. Jenny Fielding's Keep My Pipeline Flowing spreadsheet is a great resource. This is a good primer on how to prepare for funding. Do a lot of research into which funds are a good fit for you. Go to Crunchbase and see what companies they have invested in. You want investors who are interested in your space but don't have a competitive company in their portfolio. Don't waste time with investors who have a competitive company. They are mostly evaluating you for information rather than as an investment opportunity.

Talk with other entrepreneurs about what investors they know. Understand that everyone's experience is different and that a negative experience between a company and an investor may not be the same for you. Do watch out for the particularly terrible investor stories or patterns that find entrepreneurs wasting their time with certain investors.

Get your investor list, pitch, financials, and fundraising plan together. Find people to introduce you to investors and get to know them. See where you may fit.

You may only have one conversation with an investor, so go for it and see if they want to invest. This is not like dating where you need to warm up and ask about their investment interest on a third date. You may not get to the third conversation so take the opportunity to ask when you can. Ask for commitment and look for their doubts and concerns. Remedy their doubts and concerns. When someone does show interest, act fast, and don't let it go away.

The following table provides a side-by-side comparison of angels and VC investors. These are general terms and vary based on industry, location, market conditions, and investor personalities.

	ANGEL INVESTOR	VENTURE CAPITAL INVESTOR
Definition	Typically a high-net-worth individual who invests in companies they are interested in	Investor who deploys large sums of cash pooled from many investors, usually around an industry focus
Amount invested	$10k–500k	$500k+
Investment stage	Seed, startup	Seed through growth
Involvement	Low	High, often with board representation
Exit expectations	Often aligned with founders	Focus on high returns, usually through IPO or acquisition
Ownership stake	Typically smaller	Typically larger
Flexibility	Typically more flexible	More standardized terms
Relationships	Personal connections	Network of investors

In your funding journey, consider revenue, grants, angel funding, and venture capital.

34
FUNDING

How much $ do I need? _____

What am I going to do with it? _____

Which milestones will it get me to? _____

When I successfully reach a milestone, what do I do? _____

CAN I START TO MAKE MONEY NOW? CAN I GET AN ADVANCE PAYMENT?

- **YES** → YOU KNOW WHAT TO DO! FOCUS YOUR EFFORTS ON SALES. CHECK OUT REVENUE-BASED FINANCING ONCE YOU GET GOING.
- **NO** → CAN I GO FOR GRANT FUNDING?
  - **YES** → GO FOR IT! NON-DILUTIVE FUNDING IS GREAT!
  - **NO** → DO I NEED MORE THAN 1 ROUND OF FUNDING?
    - **YES** → DO I HAVE A PROVEN PRODUCT, EVIDENCE OF SALES TRACTION, A HUGE MARKET, AND A FUNDING TEAM THAT INCLUDES WHAT VCS ARE LOOKING FOR?
      - **NO** → EXPLORE VENTURE CAPITAL FUNDING
      - **YES** → EXPLORE ANGEL FUNDING TO FILL THE HOLES TO GET YOU TO VENTURE FUNDING
    - **NO** → SEEK ANGEL FUNDING

Template Notes

You can download a printable version of this template at: makeopportunityhappen.com/templates/34

Answer the top **questions** to get a handle on your funding needs and what you'll do with the funding you receive. Then follow the **flowchart** to consider your different options and plan your funding strategy. Use this guide when you first get started and at each milestone you reach.

RECAP

The top four ways to use funding to align your stars:

1. Know that for many of us, funding is one of the most challenging parts of starting a business. But entrepreneurs find a way.
2. Consider federal grant funding if you can align your product development with federal agencies' interests. Whenever you can get client revenue, that provides validation that customers want what you are offering.
3. Pursue angel funding when you need one round of financing and then can grow organically or need an initial round to get to venture capital. Pursue VC funding when you have a model with extremely high growth potential and repeat investment rounds.
4. Use Template 34 to think through your funding strategy.

RESOURCES

- *Venture Deals, 4th Edition: Be Smarter than Your Lawyer and Venture Capitalist* by Brad Feld, Jason Mendelson, et al.

- Raise Money with David Cohen: https://www.youtube.com/watch?v=xrPQOMxvuz8
- Startup Hacks by Alex Iskold: https://www.startuphacks.vc/
- AngelList: angellist.com/startups
- Y Combinator Safe Financing Documents: ycombinator.com/documents/
- Jenny Fielding's Keep Your Funding Flowing: https://www.slideshare.net/jefielding/building-an-investor-pipeline-spreadsheet-keep-your-funding-flowing
- *Angel Investing: The Gust Guide to Making Money and Having Fun Investing in Startups* by David S. Rose and Gildan Media, LLC
- *Secrets of Sand Hill Road: Venture Capital and How to Get It* by Scott Kupor, Eric Ries, et al.
- Omnicalculator: omnicalculator.com/finance/pre-and-post-money-valuation
- Visible: https://visible.vc/
- *Invest Like the Best with Patrick O'Shaughnessy* podcast

✳ ✳ ✳

Whether in your funding journey or otherwise, you can get stuck, even with the best-laid plans. The ability to get unstuck is important in your Perseverance Constellation. Let's talk about strategies for getting unstuck when it happens.

METHOD 35

Get Unstuck

"I can't change the direction of the wind, but I can adjust my sails to always reach my destination."

—JIMMY DEAN

WHEN WE STARTED ORBIS, WE FOCUSED ON FOUR AREAS: pharmaceuticals, consumer products, specialty chemicals, and food and beverages. It was the end of 2008, and the economy was nosediving. We needed our angel funding to last as long as possible, so we leaned into early client revenue as much as possible. This provided cash AND the learning to get to product-market-fit. We hypothesized that if we could establish enough proof of concept in, for example, agrochemicals, then perhaps Monsanto would license the technology for that field of use.

We finished a three-month flavor-change project with a large gum manufacturer. When we presented our problems to the client, the thirty-year-seasoned veteran said, "I wondered if you were going to figure that out." I realized it was too big of an ask for our team to know everything about our technology and all these industries. After that moment, we focused on the pharmaceutical industry.

You can say, "Of course, you should have focused! You could see that a mile away!" Well, what if we were right, and a proof-of-concept project would have been enough to license the technology for agrochemicals to Monsanto? You never know until you try.

We tried it. We learned. We moved on.

Far more often, you get stuck analyzing *Which is the best industry? How should we approach it?* The market will answer those questions if you start. But you have to learn quickly as you go. Quick action always beats a ton of thought and is an important star in your Perseverance Constellation.

Nothing is perfect when it starts. It matters less about where you are now and more about where you are going and your progress. Keeping that in mind makes it easier to handle the disappointments.

There is a fine line between focus and having options. If you focus too narrowly, you don't have any options when a problem pops up. However, you will never cross any finish lines if you don't focus enough. There are several factors to consider. The first is, *What is the amount that you can do well?* Be honest with yourself about this, as time is always limited.

The best way to have good ideas is to have lots of them. The most common reason for not making progress is lack of focus. How do you keep the ideas flowing without getting distracted? An open culture where people feel comfortable sharing ideas helps keep ideas flowing. Have a set decision tree on how you filter the ideas that enable you to move quickly in deciding if you should pursue it or put it in a file for another time (or never!). Template 35 provides questions to organize things in buckets.

One question to ask yourself: *Is it additive or distracting?* If exploring an idea outside your focus area is additive, that could be a good exploration. If not, consider putting it in a folder for another day. Like discoveries in the gum project helped us advance our thinking in oral pharmaceuticals, you never know what you will get until you try it. However, as soon as we realized we were spreading ourselves too thin and were in the distracting zone, we created more focus.

To figure out what we wanted to pursue or not, we asked:

- Do we have a reasonable chance of success with this proof of concept?
- Can we test it quickly?
- If we are successful, does the product have a reasonable chance of getting to market?
- Given our capacity, can we ensure something with a better chance of success doesn't suffer?

If the answers were yes to all these questions, we proceeded. If there were any nos, we didn't continue. This was particularly true with the speed of the test as a proof of concept that takes two years is often death to a startup.

Balancing quality and speed is essential. You can always improve quality, but you can never recover time. Appreciating quality versus speed helps you navigate what is appropriate for each stage. You can't let one harm the other. You have to know yourself on this one. If you are a perfectionist, this one's for you. If you tend to half-ass things, don't use "Quality versus Speed" as an excuse to deliver something crappy.

It's always great to give 100 percent, but when expectations require 180 percent, it's time to reevaluate. Look at your priorities, the chance of success, deadlines, and your (and your team's) capacity. Take a page from your college final exam preparation when calculating the final test score to get a specific grade.

Shooting for 100 percent when 93 percent gets you an A makes you reconsider the extra thirty hours to get to 100 percent, especially if that time makes your other grades suffer.

One of my best mentors, Tom, ingrained in my mind, "Perfect is the enemy of good, and good is almost always good enough." This motto has helped me get many things out the door while protecting my sanity.

Other strategies include:

- **Put a task on your calendar and assign a time limit.** You can block 8:00–10:00 a.m. on Thursday to work on the client proposal. Lock yourself in your office, turn off the phone and email, switch on your best music, and focus 100 percent on the proposal. When 10:00 a.m. arrives, you either submit the proposal or make a note of what you should do next time you work on it.
- **Play the relay game.** Often, a suitable endpoint is to hand the baton to someone else. Send a draft to your colleague at the end of your push. If working alone, you can get a draft to a thought partner, coworker, friend, or peer. Even if they don't read it, it's a good urgency builder for you. But it's better if they are your partner on the mission and help you carry the load.
- **Reset your expectations.** Sometimes, you must reevaluate where you are and what you want to achieve. Reevaluating is essential when an unforeseen illness, departing employee, or pandemic pops up. As addressed in Method 31, sometimes shit happens. Revisit your priorities, chance of success, deadlines, and your team's capacity.
- **Establish your criteria.** If you are struggling with deciding, list your essential, nice to have, and extra-credit elements. This helps determine what is nonnegotiable and what is

icing on the cake to provide a framework for decisions going forward.
- **Reduce your options.** Speed is your strength. Use your criteria to help you quickly narrow your choices. Give yourself a smaller set of options to move faster.

To get unstuck, leverage "perfect is the enemy of good and good is almost always good enough." If you take action and learn quickly, the market will tell you the way to go. This is far better than thinking your company to death.

(35)
GET *unstuck*

I am here: _____   I am going: _____

| ESSENTIAL | NICE TO HAVE | EXTRA CREDIT |

TOP PRIORITY →   DO NEXT →   IF THERE'S TIME →

Template Notes

You can download a printable version of this template at: makeopportunityhappen.com/templates/35

Use this template for specific projects that you need to complete in a limited time. Outline what makes perfect and what makes good by defining your **essential, nice to have**, and **extra credit** elements. Prioritize the essential and work across the priority list from there.

RECAP

The top four ways to get unstuck to align your stars:

1. Run an experiment when you find yourself on overload (see Method 25). The market will tell you which way to go. Remember: perfect is the enemy of good, and good is almost always good enough.
2. Know that there is a line between focus and having options. If you focus too narrowly, when a problem pops up, you don't have any options. But you will never cross any finish lines if you don't focus enough.
3. Use Template 35 to determine your essential, nice-to-have, and extra credit elements. Focus on the nonnegotiables and work across the priority list from there.
4. Put a task on your calendar and assign a time limit, play the relay game, reset your expectations, or reduce your options to move faster.

RESOURCES

- *StartUp* podcast

- *The School of Greatness Podcast* by Lewis Howes

✣ ✣ ✣

Getting unstuck helps prevent a lot of stress. Avoiding the stress of not getting things done is also a skill to develop. This star in your Perseverance Constellation enables you to align stars faster with less friction. Let's go there next.

METHOD 36

Avoiding the Stress of Not Getting Things Done

"Overload is like a traffic jam; you can't move forward, you can't move backward, and you can't get out of the car."

—JEFFREY GITOMER

I REALIZED THERE WERE TOO MANY THINGS ON MY LIST when items would slide from week to week. My problem was that I could never get through an entire to-do list because it was too long. I thought, *Isn't that a win if you shoot for 150 percent and get 115 percent capacity? It's over 100 percent! What more do you want? You exceeded what is reasonable to expect. What's the problem?*

I hadn't realized the harmful effects of not getting stuff done. It wears you down and opens the door to: *Are you ever good enough? Should you be doing this?* and *Will this ever work?* The impact of carrying something for many days in a row is the mental drag of not getting something done. That is the danger of having too long of a list. For sure, I have big plans. But day to day, I have a reasonable list.

When you get overwhelmed, you must reassess your list

and schedule to find room to breathe. How do you do that? Prioritize. Delegate. Cross stuff off. In this long game, these are stars in your Perseverance Constellation.

When you get to this place, ask yourself these questions:

- *Does this really need to get done?*
- *Does this really need to get done by me?*

If the answer is yes to both questions, do it now or block time on the calendar to complete it. Rip the Band-Aid. It's just weighing you down. If the answer is no to either question, delete it or delegate it. If it's questionable, move it to the "Do it later, maybe" list. Tap your future self and move stuff off your list, knowing you can revisit it sometime in the future.

Entrepreneurs have a crazy number of things they need to get done. When ordering your list, the first question is, *What is the most important thing that needs to be done now?* Sometimes, there are fast things you can get done that provide good momentum. There may be things that are weighing you down that you dread, and you've let go too long. Getting those done frees you to go on and focus on other things.

Sometimes, delivering something to someone else is what you need to move it along. One task may be number three or four on your list. If you need to get someone information so they can do their job, it becomes number one. Then, they are working on that item while you work on other priorities.

Set a top three list for yourself. When you decide on the top three, ask yourself:

- *How important is it?*
- *Does someone else need it?*
- *How long does it take?*

The answers to these questions help you establish your top three list. Do your top three things at the beginning of the day. Then, the rest of what you get done that day is a bonus.

If a task remains on your to-do list at the end of the week, ask yourself:

- *Do I really need to do it?* If items on the list are not top priority but are difficult to delete, use the "Maybe Later" list. You hardly ever bring anything back from my "Maybe Later" list to your actual to-do list, but you always have the option.
- *Am I making it more complex than it needs to be?* You often see another path forward if you challenge your assumptions or look at it differently.
- *Am I letting a hurdle stop me from finishing it?* You are often on hold for something (e.g., waiting for the client to return from vacation or an employee to start). Do you need to wait for it, or can you begin something to keep the momentum going? Watch for the things that become an excuse and let you or your team comfortably stay paused.
- *How can I chunk it?* Can you decouple it? (See Method 6.)
- *Do I need to reset expectations?* If so, remember perfect is the enemy of good. Get to an endpoint and move on. (See Method 35.)
- *Am I the best person to do this, or can I delegate it?* Is delaying getting it done a sign that you shouldn't be the one doing it?
- *Can I delegate if moving things off the list isn't an option?* This is when you say, *Wait! There is no one to delegate to.* Challenge yourself to think creatively. Can you hand it over to your kids, spouse/partner, outsourced help, virtual assistant, or even a future you? Brainstorm a "Give it to someone else" list and have the list handy. Sometimes, there are more options than you let yourself think about.

If things you need to do are not reaching your list, check that you have:

- **A way to capture what you need to get done.** This can be through a list on your phone, paper, or computer. Have one place to capture it, preferably something that's always with you.
- **A method to process it.** For example, go through the week's notes on Fridays and add items to your to-do list, calendar events, and follow-up list. Otherwise, the next thing you know, you have 200 notes that aren't helpful anymore.
- **A discipline to avoid the "Whatever happened to _____" problem.** Fill in the blank with anything: that stuff you ordered, that person getting back to you, or that introduction she promised you. Have a follow-up list and a system. It keeps you from waking up in the middle of the night in a panic because things are slipping through the cracks.
- **Weekly meetings with a preset template.** Add to the template throughout the week, and then discuss each point with your team on Monday. It keeps you accountable, helps you roll tasks through each week, and gives you the checklist you need to do.

Use whatever method works for you. Just have a system and manage it. There are lots of tools for this. If we include them here, the list will be outdated when you read this.

Also, be careful if your weekend to-do lists are remarkably optimistic. Think about the weekend list through this lens:

- What would you be glad you crossed off the list on Sunday at 10:00 p.m.? This covers the practical part of the list (e.g., that refrigerator isn't going to clean itself).

- What would you be glad you did if you died tomorrow? This covers the what-really-matters-in-life part of the list (e.g., spending time with family).

Be sure to put the fun stuff on your calendar, from walking with a friend to getting ice cream with your kids. It's more likely to happen when it's on your calendar. This is for short thirty- to sixty-minute items and longer reset items. I have a standing time at 7:00 a.m. on the second Sunday of every month to walk with one of my best college friends. We wouldn't see each other as often if we weren't intentional. Get it on the calendar.

Revisiting this mantra, "Do what you say. Say what you mean." The philosophy also applies to yourself. Don't cheat yourself. If you take the day off, take the day off. If you say you'll work out for sixty minutes, work out for sixty minutes. You may want to stop at minute fifty-eight and round up. Seeing sixty on the clock is satisfying and reinforces that you are someone who gets it done!

Don't put things on your list that don't belong there. Follow a structured process to rapidly think through what goes on your list or in another bucket for another time or person.

avoid the *stress* OF NOT GETTING THINGS DONE

WHAT ARE MY TOP 3 GOALS?
- Is it important to the progress of my business?
- Do I have a near-term deadline?
- Will it move me closer to money in the bank?
- Will it relieve a big worry or fear?
- What will I be most satisfied to say is done at the end of the day?

1. _____
2. _____
3. _____

FOR EACH ITEM ON YOUR LIST, ASK YOURSELF:
IS IT IMPORTANT TO MEET MY TOP 3 GOALS?

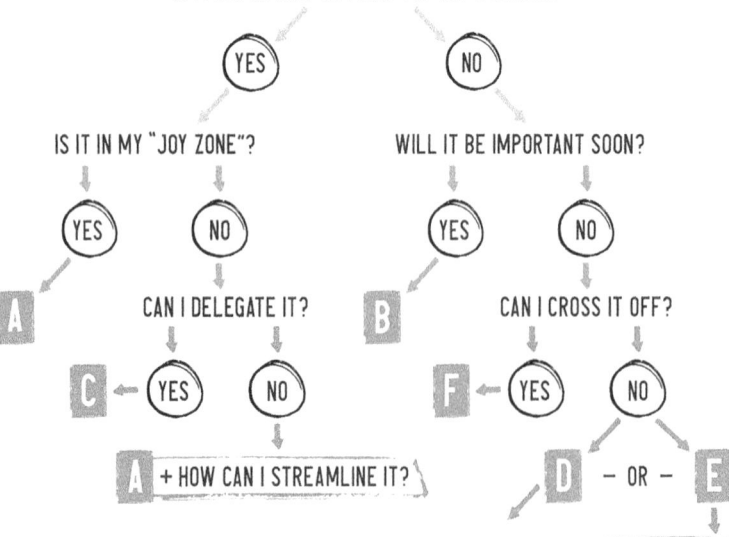

- **YES** → IS IT IN MY "JOY ZONE"?
  - **YES** → **A**
  - **NO** → CAN I DELEGATE IT?
    - **YES** → **C**
    - **NO** → **A** + HOW CAN I STREAMLINE IT?
- **NO** → WILL IT BE IMPORTANT SOON?
  - **YES** → **B**
  - **NO** → CAN I CROSS IT OFF?
    - **YES** → **F**
    - **NO** → **D** I'LL DO IT LATER — OR — **E** I'LL CONSIDER DOING IT LATER

A TODAY! | **B** NEAR TERM | **C** DELEGATE | **D** FUTURE SELF | **E** MAYBE LATER | **F** CROSS OFF

Template Notes

You can download a printable version of this template at: makeopportunityhappen.com/templates/36

Start with the top section, distilling your **top three goals** by answering the questions. As you decide to take on new things, use the **decision tree** to determine what goes on your today, near-term, delegate, future-self, and maybe-later buckets. Everything else lands in the cross-off bucket.

RECAP

The top four ways to avoid the stress of not getting things done to align your stars:

1. Ask yourself: *Does this **need** to get done? Do I need to do it?*
2. Seek the aid of your future self. Create a "Maybe Later" folder to move stuff off your list today.
3. Revise how things get on the list in the first place. Use the Template 36 decision tree to help you decide what goes on your list or gets crossed off. Let your goals be your guiding beacons.
4. Be sure to put the fun stuff on your calendar.

RESOURCES

- *Boundaries Updated and Expanded Edition: When to Say Yes, How to Say No To Take Control of Your Life* by Henry Cloud and John Townsend
- *Getting Things Done: The Art of Stress-Free Productivity* by David Allen and James Fallows

- *Deep Work: Rules for Focused Success in a Distracted World* by Cal Newport, Jeff Bottoms, et al.

※ ※ ※

Now that you are realistic about what you can do in a given time period, focus on what is most important. Doing what fills you up helps you turbocharge your efforts because you are operating in your sweet spot. Let's explore this star in your Perseverance Constellation next.

METHOD 37

What Fills You Up

"Don't ask yourself what the world needs. Ask yourself what makes you come alive and then go do that. Because what the world needs is people who have come alive."

—HOWARD THURMAN

AFTER SELLING ORBIS AND HAVING THE FREEDOM TO choose what to do next, I did a lot of self-reflection on what fills me up. I read many books, watched talks, and listened to podcasts in search of the answers. I take pride in being a capable person who can do a lot of things. So when I see something and say to myself, *I can do that*, I go to my list of things that fill me up, and it guides me to pursue it or not.

When navigating the entrepreneurs' waters, you need lots of energy. There will be many times when you question if you should be doing this. Two things that help you are: (1) a deep connection to the mission of what you are doing and (2) understanding what fills you up versus what drains you. Understand how to do more of what gives you energy while delegating what drains you. Finding the intersection of what you love to do with what the world wants you to do puts you in a place to do magic.

You don't have to quit your job and join the Peace Corps if

you crave something more. Often, you can find more minor explorations to: (1) do more of what makes you feel alive and (2) do less of what depletes you. This is an important star in your Perseverance Constellation.

The first step is simply awareness of yourself. Developing self-awareness is a lifelong journey. It's the sparkle in your eye and the subject you can discuss forever. It takes time to see it. It's like when my son talks about Minecraft, and you feel this positive energy bubble from his toes to the top of his head. Notice when you get this charge when you talk about something. When you see it, you say, "Yes! That right there! I love doing that!" Put that on your "What You Love" list.

One tip is to watch what you tell people is important in your life and what they should do. I would suggest to one of my best friends that she write children's books. It took me fifteen years of encouraging her for me to realize that I was the one who was hungry to write. I didn't recognize that encouraging my friend was an indicator of what I would love to do. It's like when my son wants us to buy a sudoku book for Nana's birthday, and he uses the book for the first forty-five minutes after Nana opens the present. If you encourage something for someone else, ask yourself if it's something for you.

After you know what makes you happy, the second exercise is to know your "I Don't Do" list. What are the things that drain your energy? Fill in the following sentence with your top three to five "I don't do _____." I don't do assholes, politics, repetitive administrative tasks, and technical problems. "I don't do assholes" helped me decide, *Should I join this team? Wait, no, I don't do assholes.* Having a list of things you love and don't do helps you make quicker, better decisions.

It's the intersection of what you love doing and what the world wants you to do. It's the best use of your genius, and the world rewards you by wanting more. The word "Ikigai" in Japanese guides you:

> Ikigai (ee-key-guy) is a Japanese concept that combines the terms iki, meaning "alive" or "life," and gai, meaning "benefit" or "worth." When combined, these terms mean that which gives your life worth, meaning, or purpose.[14]
>
> Ikigai is the intersection of these elements:

- What you love
- What you're good at
- What you can be paid for
- What the world needs

This is your genius zone. As a leader, you want to identify the genius zones of those around you and help them to thrive in that zone. Find what fills them up and help them find ways to do more of it. Find what depletes them and help them find ways to do less of it. Luckily, we are all different, and there is someone for every task. Helping people to do more of what fills them up is a gift you can give your teammates and colleagues.

There are tools to help you and your team get better self-awareness of your strengths and communication styles. These personality tests make everyone groan because it puts you in a box. These tools don't get it 100 percent correct, but if you can get an 80 percent insight, it's well worth doing. These tools include the Culture Index, Predictive Index, DiSC, Truity, and

---

14 Erin Eatough, "What Is Ikigai and How Can It Change My Life?," *BetterUp* (blog), May 7, 2021, https://www.betterup.com/blog/what-is-ikigai.

many other options. Find the right coach to help you interpret the results and what you can do with the information.

A friend joined a new team, and she and her two colleagues took a test and received coaching based on their results. They learned about the best ways to communicate and work with each other. After working with her colleagues for a year, my friend described the test results and coaching. She said, "You wouldn't believe it," then paused. I interjected, "They were right, weren't they?" My friend said, "Spot on." These tools give you a deeper understanding of yourself and others, strategies to work with each other better, and maps to your energy sources and drains.

Doing what fills you up gives you lots of energy and superpowers. Take time to figure out and spend more time in your genius zone.

WHAT *fills* YOU UP

(37)

ENERGY SOURCES

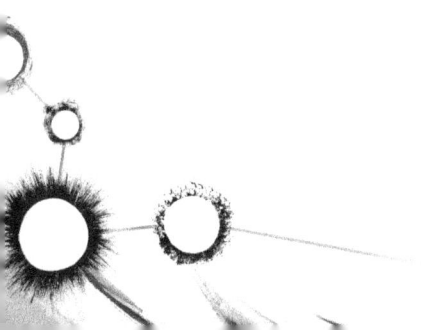

ACTIVITY	HOW TO GET MORE	NEXT STEP

ENERGY DRAINS

ACTIVITY	DELEGATE	NEXT STEP

Template Notes

You can download a printable version of this template at: makeopportunityhappen.com/templates/37

In the top section, list the **activities** that give you energy. How can you **get more** of these things in your life? Is it in your work, volunteering, or hobbies? What are the immediate **next steps** to help you do this?

In the bottom section, list the **activities** that drain you. How can you have fewer of these things in your life? Can you **delegate, automate**, or **just stop** doing them? What are the immediate **next steps** to do that?

RECAP

The top four ways to do what fills you up to align your stars:

1. Understand that self-awareness is the key to knowing how to:
   A. Do more of what makes you feel alive.
   B. Do less of what depletes you.
2. Use Template 37 to help you distill your sources and drains and get more of your energy sources and less of your energy drains.
3. Find the intersection of what you love doing and what the world wants you to do. This is your "What I Love" list that puts you in a place to do magic.
4. Know your "I Don't Do" list. What are the things that drain your energy?

RESOURCES

- *Designing Your Life: How to Build a Well-Lived, Joyful Life* by Bill Burnett and Dave Evans
- Sparketype: goodlifeproject.com/podcast/sparketypes/
- The 23 Best Personality Tests In Ranking Order https://www.workstyle.io/best-personality-test

※ ※ ※

One of the things you want to avoid is the *"Long in the Tooth" Syndrome*. You want to dodge that black hole. Your Perseverance Constellation requires you to know what this syndrome is and have strategies to avoid getting sucked in.

METHOD 38

The "Long in the Tooth" Syndrome

"Believe in yourself and all that you are. Know that there is something inside you that is greater than any obstacle."

—CHRISTIAN D. LARSON

PEOPLE CALL ME BECAUSE THEY KNOW I HAVE BEEN THERE, and they say, "I've been working on my startup for eight years. Should I be doing this? Is this worth it?" I get this call a lot. It's after something particularly shitty or a string of shitty things happens, and you don't know if you should keep going. Everything is so hard, and everything is taking so long.

When I told a group of entrepreneur peers the Orbis story, one man said, "So before you got Long in the Tooth..." It was a booming sound "LOOOONG IN THE TOOOTH!" What! What a horrible thing to say! But it was fitting. *"Long in the Tooth" Syndrome* is when your company is feeling old.

How do you keep your business from getting "Long in the Tooth"? This is when you continually ask yourself, *Should I be doing this? Is this worth it?*

We get down but have to have a way to get back up. To help you with this star in your Perseverance Constellation, Method

38 provides a roadmap to getting back up and finding that motivation or moving on to something different.

Sometimes, you wake up tomorrow, the storm clouds disappear, and there is reason to keep going. Sometimes, the funding comes in, the client says yes, a regulation changes, or the salesperson starts selling. The world is constantly changing. Sometimes, people wake up and "boom," their company is ready to seize the opportunity.

Timing is such a big part of the game. The voice of Cerner's CEO, Neal Patterson, would be in my head saying, *Timing is everything. If you're too early, you're dead. If you're too late, you're irrelevant. This is the third time I'm working on this part.* That third time was when I got to ride on the spaceship, and we made a lot of progress.

Sometimes, it's market timing, and you must keep going. Sometimes, you need a vacation. Sometimes, you take what you learned and move on. How do you know when to keep going, take a vacation, or move on? This is one of the hardest things about being an entrepreneur, so let's create a framework for thinking about it.

Let's start with the easiest first: vacation. How long has it been since you have had a vacation? A real vacation? What have you been through the last three to six to twelve months? Besides the heartbreak with your business, people go through divorces, moves, deaths, health traumas, and financial distress. Often, they don't stop to take a break. They just move through it. When you have had these incredibly stressful things happen, consider taking a vacation. I'm not saying a week at the beach is all the repair you need, but it could be a place to start.

Go somewhere that will rejuvenate you, with people who will renew you (and sometimes that is just you), for the time that will refresh you. See how you feel about getting back into things when you return. That helps judge if you need to hit the reset button or do something else. Often, when you are not thinking about it, you get perspective and can make a list of adjustments that will help make life better.

When deciding if you should just keep going or if you can make a shift, consider these questions:

- Where is your company going?
- Does your company give you energy?
- What are your other options?

Have an honest evaluation of these questions and revisit the questions quarterly to see trends. Are you down because that crappy thing happened, or have you felt this way for the last three years?

The entrepreneur's job is to have insight and vision into the future, to learn and adapt when new information arises. An investor told me we need to get better at pulling the plug earlier and stop funding things that don't go anywhere. I said, "How do you know?" There are many examples of things that need to marinate for a while and timing that needs to ripen, and then—boom—their company is a rocket ship. Remember Melanie and the Canva story?

Conversely, sometimes shutting something down allows for something better to arise. You only have so much energy. Stop doing things that don't have a chance.

It's hard to keep going when it's not fun anymore. When you feel like a cat on its fifteenth life, you must realize when to plow through versus jump ship. Time kills all deals. Time kills all spirits. Protect your time and, thus, your spirit.

It's easy to say "pull the plug" as an outsider. But it's super tricky when you are in the middle of it. You can see the frenzy that the word "pivot" can create. "Oh, this is so hard. If I just pivot this way. No, that way. Wait! It's this way!" You are looking for the magic formula that will make things take off. Sometimes, you just need to stay the course.

The pivot is often talked about, but rarely do you talk about how difficult and sometimes damaging it is. Commonly seen as the overall solution to your problems, it can be to your detriment. Knowing when to pivot is critical. Build a culture of small pivots and fail fast. Make minor adjustments and avoid large ruts requiring a huge pivot.

To get your star back in place, have people you can talk to, such as your:

- Co-founder
- Peer entrepreneurs who have been there and can offer you their perspective
- Mentor, coach, or therapist (or all three)
- Spouse or close confidantes

Beyond your sounding board and support system, the antidotes to this long-in-the-tooth feeling are gratitude and having a strong sense of why. Even in the darkest times, you can still find things to be grateful for, which can be what you need to rebound. A strong sense of why is: (1) a profound belief in your technology or service and (2) a deep confidence in yourself and your team. You are the people to bring this product to the world.

If you decide there isn't enough evidence to keep going or you are just at the end of your rope, that is OK. Think about what you learned to serve as a springboard to the next thing. The new path forward is in the story you tell, and you must believe the story yourself before telling others. Often, there is something great just around the corner. The grass is always greener, but sometimes it's good to stand on a different lawn.

The "Long in the Tooth" Syndrome is when your business is getting old, where you continually ask yourself, *Should I be doing this?* You get down but have to have a way to get back up. It's about finding motivation or moving on to something different, if necessary.

the LONG IN THE TOOTH *syndrome*

QUESTION	YOUR ANSWER	STAY THE COURSE	MAKE A CHANGE
What is your company's current state?		☐	☐
What progress have you made so far?		☐	☐
Is your company making money, and is it enough to sustain the business and grow?		☐	☐
How big is your market, really (now that you know more)?		☐	☐
Do you have a scalable business model? What proof do you have?		☐	☐
Do you have a clear path to profitability?		☐	☐
Is this the team that is going to get you there?		☐	☐
Do you have funding options?		☐	☐
Do you still have the drive to fulfill your company's vision?		☐	☐
Are there other opportunities you're interested in pursuing, and how do they compare to what you're doing now?		☐	☐

Template Notes

You can download a printable version of this template at: makeopportunityhappen.com/templates/38

Answer these questions to journal your thoughts and give yourself a guide for whether you should **stay the course** or **make a change**. If you get stuck, think through quick experiments you could run to test theories and help you decide.

RECAP

The top four ways to prevent the "Long in the Tooth" Syndrome to align your stars:

1. Consider if a vacation or another way to reset can help you.
2. Lean into gratitude and have a solid sense of why as an antidote to feeling down.
3. Have people you can talk to, including a co-founder, peer entrepreneurs, mentor, coach, therapist, spouse, or confidante (or all of the above!).
4. Use Template 38 to assess your situation. Know when to keep going, go on vacation, or take what you learned and move on.

RESOURCES

- *The Magic of Surrender: Finding the Courage to Let Go* by Kute Blackson
- "The Power of Time Off," a TED Talk by Stefan Sagmeister
- "The Art of Stillness," a TED Talk by Pico Iyer

* * *

Regardless of whether you get the "Long in the Tooth" Syndrome, know that you are playing a long game. That is why your Perseverance Constellation is so critical. You need to understand how to continually get *Your Next Wind*.

METHOD 39

Your Next Wind

"Our greatest glory is not in never falling, but in rising every time we fall."

—CONFUCIUS, OLIVER GOLDSMITH, NELSON MANDELA, VINCE LOMBARDI, RALPH WALDO EMERSON (EVEN THE GREATS TOOK A PAGE FROM EACH OTHER)

AT ORBIS, WE HAD BEEN WORKING WITH A KEY CUSTOMER for a few years. We were making progress, and it seemed like this client would take us to the promised land. This client would be the first to market a product that used our technology, laying the path for other companies to follow. We were chipping away at the important milestones. Then, one day, the client said they had an internal disagreement on what projects to take forward. Another part of their organization won. They were shutting down our product.

While we had other clients and other opportunities, this was the big one! The loss of this client was a gut punch. It took the wind out of our sails (and out of our sales). Whatever words you want to use, it sucked. We lost a key leader on our team because it was so heartbreaking. It's just not how the world should work. You do your part and should be able to keep going, right? Unfortunately, this isn't the way it goes sometimes.

If your entrepreneurial journey looks anything like mine, you make progress up the mountain, and then you fall and slide down the mountain. You progress up the mountain, then you stumble and lose a few steps. You make progress up the mountain, and then you have a massive fall down the mountain. Eventually, you reach the summit, see the next mountain to climb, and start climbing *that* mountain.

All this stumbling and sliding down the mountain wears you down. This is the time when you dig deep for your second wind. While we give a cat nine lives, sometimes I felt like I was on my fifteenth life. Forget the *second* wind. You need to keep digging deep into the motivation and energy well for *Your Next Wind* when things are tough. Your Next Wind is renewing yourself and getting back up and is perhaps the most critical star in your Perseverance Constellation.

We've already determined that you are playing a long game. Hopefully, you are getting enough of the "This is working!" green-light signals to balance out the "Why is everything a crisis?" speed-bump moments.

Sometimes, things draw out so long, and you grind, grind, and grind. Then, there is one (or more) terrible event(s), and you don't know if you should keep going. The Next Wind is renewing yourself to get back up and keep going. This is an important skill to put things in perspective, get yourself back in the action, and rally your team. This helps keep your people engaged, motivated, and going in the same direction.

Sometimes, you need to hit the reset button. You need a vacation (see Method 38), a retreat, dinner with a good friend, or a long bath. Do these things regularly. Think about the more minor things that you can do daily and weekly. You forget about that. Daily: sleep well, exercise, eat well, and be around people who lift you. Weekly: reading, tennis, a movie, or what works for you. Examine your routines and habits. What are the routines that are serving you that you want to keep going or increase, and what are the routines that need a change?

Think about how you can change your environment. Be in a place that makes you feel good and allows you to do what you need to do. Be around people who inspire you and give you good ideas. If you don't have the positive energy right now, rely on others' energy until you get yours. Often co-founders can pass the baton back and forth. One of your goals is that you both can't be at rock bottom at the same time. When one founder goes there, the other must be ready to pull them up and vice versa.

Focus on your spiritual foundation: why you do what you do. The bigger vision of who you are helps you put things into perspective. It helps you to not care about things you shouldn't care about and focus on what matters the most.

Renewing yourself and getting back up for more means taking the needed break and then focusing on the good, what you can do, and what is working. If you keep chipping away at it, the world catches up with you, and better days are ahead.

Sometimes, you need a change in what you are doing or how the team is doing it. Make sure you are doing the right things and not letting perfect be the enemy of good. Maintain focus and give yourself regular resets and reinforcements. When things aren't working or you are down, stressed, or fearful, get to the root of things. Reflecting in stillness and talking with others helps to see what is at the heart of things.

If you are wondering about that client who stopped working with us, they came back around and became a long-standing partner. You never know what tomorrow brings.

GETTING YOUR *next* WIND

HIT THE RESET BUTTON
- **Overwhelmed and stressed?** If you're constantly playing catchup or have too many tasks and responsibilities, take a step back and reassess your priorities.
- **Lack of motivation?** If it's difficult to get started on things you used to enjoy, take a break and recharge.
- **Loss of focus and direction?** Reflect on your values and priorities.
- **Unfulfilled or unhappy?** Evaluate what changes to make.
- **Physical and mental health problems?** Prioritize your well-being and seek help.

CHANGE YOUR ENVIRONMENT, SUCH AS YOUR:
- **Physical environment.** Change your physical surroundings, get some fresh air, go for a walk, or rearrange your workspace.
- **Social environment.** Surround yourself with positive and supportive people to feel more motivated and inspired.
- **Work environment.** Reduce distractions, delegate tasks, or rework your workload.
- **Mental environment.** Practice mindfulness, meditation, or other relaxation techniques.

EVALUATE ROUTINES AND HABITS, SUCH AS YOUR:
- **Sleep.** Adjust your sleep schedule to feel more alert and productive.
- **Exercise and/or diet.** Stay active to boost your energy levels, reduce stress, and improve your overall well-being.
- **Mindfulness.** Practice mindfulness even for a few minutes a day to feel more calm and focused.
- **Task prioritization.** Focus on your most important items to get back on track.

MAKE A CHANGE WHEN:
- **You can't find a way forward,** or you are chronically unhappy, unfulfilled, or unsatisfied.
- **Other stars are aligning that you can't pass up** as new opportunities present themselves.
- **Your other priorities are suffering,** such as your health or relationships and you can't find a way to improve.

Template Notes

You can download a printable version of this template at: makeopportunityhappen.com/templates/39

Consider these **questions** when deciding whether to **stay the course** or **adjust** your strategy. Think through changes you can make to your environment, routines, or habits.

RECAP

The top four ways to get Your Next Wind to align your stars:

1. Understand that the entrepreneurial journey often resembles a repeated loop of making progress and sliding down the mountain.
2. Get to the root of things when things aren't working or you are down, stressed, or fearful.
3. Reflect in stillness and talk with others to see what is at the root of things.
4. Use Template 39 to think through hitting the reset button; changing your environment, evaluating routines and habits; and making a change.

RESOURCES

- *Shoe Dog: A Memoir by the Creator of Nike* by Phil Knight, Norbert Leo Butz, et al.
- *Find Your Why: A Practical Guide for Discovering Purpose for You and Your Team* by Simon Sinek, David Mead, et al.
- *Adversity Quotient: Turning Obstacles into Opportunities* by Paul G. Stoltz

- *Thriving in the Storm: 9 Principles to Help You Overcome Any Adversity* by Bill Murphy

※ ※ ※

One of the most important things in getting Your Next Wind is leaning on others. This is the last star in your Perseverance Constellation and in your *Make Opportunity Happen* journey! Let's close with the critical method of how other people help you align your stars.

METHOD 40

Leaning on Others

"Find your tribe, and never let them go."
—GRU FROM *THE RISE OF GRU*

WHEN I PLAY THE MOVIE OF MY LIFE IN MY HEAD, THERE are many rock-solid tribes. These tribes were most helpful when I was down, and they picked me up. When I was winning, they celebrated with me. It's also when they were down, and I got to give them a hand to stand back up. When they were winning, I celebrated with them. That is the thing with tribes—you give, and you receive. The more you put into it, the more you get out of it. You are there for them, and they are there for you. If you don't have both things happening, it isn't the right tribe for you.

In grad school, I was very down and just wanted to move on to the next phase of life. On my birthday, my lab group met to grind out a never-ending project in the computer lab. We had so much to do; graduation was in sight, so we were ready to move on. When I got to the computer lab, my teammates said, "Did you think we wouldn't know it was your birthday? We're not working on your birthday! We are going to a movie." They might as well have said they were buying me a car. I was so happy they remembered me and we were doing something other than that project.

The movie was *Sliding Doors*, where Gwyneth Paltrow plays Helen, who gets fired from her job and misses her train. Helen goes back and forth on what her life would be like if she had made the train and if she hadn't. It's fascinating how things can change based on one event. The movie is particularly thought-provoking when you think about how your decisions lead you down one path or another. You only get to pick one path. You'll never know what going down the other path would have been like.

What you do know about your path is how important the people around you are. It's your tribe: the group of peers that gives you inspiration, support, and ideas. And you offer them inspiration, support, and ideas. They know what you are going through, and you know what they are going through. You help each other feel like you are not alone. These are the people you can learn from and who can help you. You can pick each other up when you're down. You can ask the hard questions no one else asks. You can do reality checks and get tips to save time.

In college, the percentage of female engineering students was low, and we banded together to help each other. We studied together, gave each other pep talks, and pulled each other up when we were tempted to find an easier college major.

As an entrepreneur, I found my tribe in the Pipeline Entrepreneurs, a group of high-growth founders. It's a group that pushes and is there for each other. We celebrate each other's wins and share each other's pains.

Some of us feel we can go alone and don't need anyone else, so we miss the chance to walk with these people. It's not just what they can do for you. It's also what you can do for them.

Intertwining ourselves creates the rich fabric needed to align your stars in the Perseverance Constellation.

Some tribes form through an organization, and others form organically as people meet each other. In the example of my engineering department and my entrepreneurial fellowship, we raised our hands to say I am a female engineer or a high-growth entrepreneur, and we found other people raising their hands too.

How do you find the right people at the right time?

Step one is to see them. Find people willing to give advice, connections, time, and support. Find the people who are real and transparent.

Step two is to nurture the relationship. How do you keep it going instead of letting it become a memory? Find easy ways to stay connected—text chains, periodic check-ins, and sharing something that inspires you.

Step three is to appreciate it. Your tribe is such a gift. Finding each other and sharing these parts of your journeys makes for a rich life.

Leaning on others is embracing your tribe to provide and receive inspiration, support, and ideas. See them, nurture them, and appreciate them.

IMPORTANCE OF *tribe*

GO–TO MENTOR	GO TO FOR THIS EXPERTISE	KEEP UPDATED BY	APPRECIATE THEM BY

MY PEOPLE	GO TO FOR THIS EXPERTISE	KEEP UPDATED BY	APPRECIATE THEM BY

Template Notes

You can download a printable version of this template at: makeopportunityhappen.com/templates/40

Create a map of people to go to when you need advice, support, or expertise. Write down your **go-to mentor** and list the **people** in your tribe, what **expertise** they offer, how you keep them **updated**, and how you **appreciate** them. Additionally, note how often you connect with them, and reflect on whether or not you're connecting with these people as often as you need.

RECAP

The top four ways to lean on others to align your stars:

1. Know that tribes are the people you give to and you receive from. The more you put into it, the more you get out of it.
2. Rely on your tribe for inspiration, support, and ideas.
3. Find your tribe, look for them, nurture them, and appreciate them.
4. Use Template 40 to create a map of your tribe with notes on when to go to them, how to keep them updated, and ways to appreciate them.

RESOURCES

- "The Art of Asking," a TED Talk by Amanda Palmer
- *The Power of Strangers: The Benefits of Connecting in a Suspicious World* by Joe Keohane, Jonathan Todd Ross, et al.
- *Don't Be a Stranger: Create Your Own Luck in Business through Strategic Relationship Building* by Lawrence R. Perkins

✳ ✳ ✳

Your tribe is so important to helping you align your stars. Find it, nurture it, and take care of it.

Congratulations! You have made it through the Perseverance Constellation. Let's recap the journey we just took together.

CONCLUSION

Welcome, Shooting Star

AT THE ONE-YEAR MARK OF ORBIS BIOSCIENCES, WE LOOKED back at all we had accomplished. We had achieved an incredible amount of work on a lean team. We had client contracts, operations, a sales machine, and our rocket ship with great people. The entrepreneurial skills I learned growing up and in my early jobs gave me the mindset, execution, support, adaptability, and perseverance to brave the journey. I continued to hone these methods, and now, as I work with entrepreneurs, I see the need for the same methods that propelled our Orbis success.

Many of us struggle with these questions:

- Where do I really need to be in twelve months?
- How can I make more progress faster before I run out of time and money?
- How do I form the right team to get us there?
- How do I keep the team going during the down times?
- How do I keep *myself* going during the down times?

While the answers to these questions are different for everyone, other entrepreneurs' stories shine a light on the journey you want to follow. Making opportunities happen for yourself requires mindset, execution, support, adaptability, and perseverance. Remember these constellations you need to align your stars.

My superpower is to simplify and get things done. I invite you to make this your superpower too. *Make Opportunity Happen* presents methods and templates for getting things done in your startup. You can "take a page" from an entrepreneur who has walked in your shoes to help you decide how you want to proceed. There is no need to take extra steps if other people have found shortcuts that you can use.

For centuries, stars have been used to predict the future. Let me predict yours. In one year, you will have incorporated these execution, support, adaptability, and perseverance methods. You will now have the mindset to propel you to align your stars. You have gone from uncertainty and feeling overwhelmed and alone, to clarity and community. By employing these templates, you can see the progress you want. You have become your own shooting star. You glow as you move through the atmosphere!

Thank you for being on the journey with me. Now it's time to put down the book and align your stars. Come back and use this as a reference guide as you hone your own methods. Check out the website makeopportunityhappen.com for the downloadable, editable forms to use as you incorporate these methods. Look for updated resources as we continue to curate the list. And finally, if you know of an aspiring entrepreneur looking to make progress, please point them to *Make Opportunity Happen*.

Before Julio Palmaz changed the world, no one took him seriously. I can relate to this, so his story sticks with me. I remember many people on my journey who didn't take me seriously, which fueled me to prove them wrong. I suspect you can relate to this too. As if by cosmic intervention, when I wrote this conclusion, my son, Teddy, came home from school with his writing homework that read, "Don't let anyone tell you what you can't do." Amen, son.

Don't let anyone tell you what you can't do. Change the world and make people take you seriously. Go *Make Opportunity Happen*!

Acknowledgments

I HAVE A LONG LIST OF PEOPLE TO THANK FOR THEIR HELP in making this book a reality. My gratitude begins with my husband, Rob Flynn, for his unwavering support and thoughtful insight. Our kids Declan, Teddy, and Remy Flynn are an ultimate source of inspiration, and I am so grateful for their enthusiasm. I give a special shoutout to my mother-in-law, Ann Flynn, who stepped up in big ways to help us grow our family and Orbis Biosciences simultaneously.

Thank you to everyone who taught me through their example, advice, books, podcasts, and presentations. My biggest thanks go to my first teachers: my parents Alan and Juanita Stecklein for my earliest entrepreneurship lessons at their businesses and around the dinner table. Thank you to my brothers Chris and AJ Stecklein for teaching me how to keep up with the boys, which is a skill I've gone on to use repeatedly.

Thanks to my Orbis Biosciences co-founders, Bo Fishback and Cory Berkland, for starting the ignition on a great rocket ship. I appreciate my wonderful mentors, Terry Shelton and Tom Fredrick, and all the brilliant people who built Orbis. I am grateful to the entrepreneurs and mentors I have worked with through Pipeline Entrepreneurs, Techstars, and my consulting firm, Ambiologix. Being in the trenches with you has been rewarding, and I'm grateful to share in your journey.

Thank you to everyone who helped me with the book, including the many authors who inspired me and illuminated the path forward. Thank you to the team at Scribe Media for your work on *Make Opportunity Happen* and all the consultants I met along the way. I am incredibly grateful to Aaron Fulk, Rebecca Harrison, and their team at Lillian James Creative for their tremendous contribution to the book cover, templates, and website.

Thank you for contributions by Monica Smith and Steven Coen. Thank you to all the wonderful beta readers, including Bradley Hopper, Brandy Archie, Brooke Mullen, Chris Sunde, Dusty Reynolds, Eliot Arnold, Emily Brown, Josh Miller, Julia Scherer, Lee Kuczewski, Maria Iliakova, Megan O'Rear, Mandy Shoemaker, Melissa Vincent, Melissa Weed, Meredith McAllister, Nick Love, Ruth Shrauner, Sarah Hill, Shoheb Punjani, and Vanessa Jupe. Your fingerprints are all over this book, and I hope you are proud of what we created in collective wisdom.

Finally, thank *you*. You have so much to do and so little time to do it. Thank you for sharing your journey with me!

—MARIA FLYNN

Printed in the USA
CPSIA information can be obtained
at www.ICGtesting.com
JSHW020819270424
61764JS00007B/8

9 781544 545479